Flowers

with a *Painterly Touch*

Flowers

with a *Painterly Touch*

Pat Wakefield, MDA

NORTH LIGHT BOOKS

CINCINNATI, OHIO

www.artistsnetwork.com

Other fine North Light Books are available from your local
bookstore, art supply store or direct from the publisher.

06 05 04 03 02   5 4 3 2 1

Library of Congress Cataloging-in-Publication Data
Wakefield, Pat.
   Flowers with a painterly touch / Pat Wakefield.
     p. cm.
   Includes index.
   ISBN 1-58180-121-1
     1. Acrylic painting--Technique. 2. Decoration and
    ornament--Plant forms. 3. Flowers in art. I. Title.

TT385 .W3397 2002
745.7'23--dc21   2001037009

Editor: Christine Doyle
Production Coordinator: John Peavler
Designer: Joanna Detz
Interior Layout Artist: Cheryl VanDeMotter
Photographers: Christine Polomsky and Al Parrish

metric conversion chart

to convert	to	multiply by
Inches	Centimeters	2.54
Centimeters	Inches	0.4
Feet	Centimeters	30.5
Centimeters	Feet	0.03
Yards	Meters	0.9
Meters	Yards	1.1
Sq. Inches	Sq. Centimeters	6.45
Sq. Centimeters	Sq. Inches	0.16
Sq. Feet	Sq. Meters	0.09
Sq. Meters	Sq. Feet	10.8
Sq. Yards	Sq. Meters	0.8
Sq. Meters	Sq. Yards	1.2
Pounds	Kilograms	0.45
Kilograms	Pounds	2.2
Ounces	Grams	28.4
Grams	Ounces	0.04

about the author

Pat Wakefield, MDA, is the author of twenty-seven books and thirty-nine painting packets for the decorative painter. Pat has taught classes at the Cambridge House in Kansas, the first decorative painting shop in the country, as well as at shops and conventions throughout the U.S. and Canada. Her paintings and articles have been included in several international publications. She studied fine art at the University of Kansas and is a long-time member of the Society of Decorative Painters for which she has been a judge in their certification program and has taught at several conventions. Pat received her Master Decorative Artist Certification in this society in 1975. She is versatile in her painting styles and techniques, painting with tube oils, acrylics, pastels and watercolors. Pat lives with her husband in the Kansas City area.

For information on Pat's seminars and publications, contact her at: Pat Wakefield, MDA, P.O. Box 3245, Shawnee Mission, KS 66203, phone: 913-649-8318, e-mail: pat@patwakefield.com or at her web site http://www.patwakefield.com.

If you are interested in decorative painting, it is very beneficial to obtain membership in the Society of Decorative Painters. This will put you in touch with the more than 30,000 worldwide members of this fine organization through their publication, *The Decorative Painter*. Many cities have local chapters that will be of benefit to you. Write to: The Society of Decorative Painters, 393 N. McLean Blvd., Wichita, KS 67203-5968 or call 316-269-9191.

table of contents

introduction

The artistic process of painting is much more involved than merely applying paint to a surface. We are influenced in our painting abilities, techniques and accomplishments by our total life experiences. Even our personality traits are evident in our painting. Are you an organized person who likes things in perfect order or are you carefree and loosely put together with little concern for details? Are your kitchen cupboards clean, neat and orderly or do you have to look for your spices behind the noodles and canned goods? We feel more comfortable painting in a style that suits us individually.

Most decorative painters begin painting either realistic designs or those that involve traditional strokework and they feel most comfortable with these styles. These styles of painting are neat and seem the easiest to accomplish. But after starting with a realistic style to get the basics, many painters get a sense of which things could be left out to make a softer, looser and more pleasing painting. A loose style is sometimes referred to as impressionistic, as that was history's big step in fine art from realism to the new Impressionists in the late 1800s. This style of painting is a rendering of the sense of the artist with little attention to detail. Much is left to the imagination of the viewer.

The floral projects in this book embrace this loose, impressionistic style. While some look more realistic than others, all are painted with quick brushstrokes that are more "painterly" than traditional decorative painting strokework. The soft and loose look is achieved using large brushes, quick strokes and mixed colors, all of which are described in detail in this book.

For some, the impressionistic style of painting will come easily. The loose, carefree strokes will fit well with a carefree personality. But for those who like order in their life and put neatness at a premium, this easy-looking style of painting may actually be the most difficult to paint.

It takes courage to move beyond the familiar into a new experience. You feel uncomfortable until you spend time developing your skill through practice and patience. Keep in mind that each person's painting will be quite different from another's, as this style is an expression of you. Your inner self will be evident and should not be compared with another's nor should you try to change.

Let yourself go and enjoy the results.

Pat Wakefield, MDA

materials

Paints

When painting the projects in this book, you can use the medium of your choice. The instructions call for Plaid's FolkArt Artists' Pigment Acrylic Paint and some FolkArt Acrylic Paint (premixed colors). But there are color swatches of all the paints and paint mixtures given with each project so you can easily substitute watercolors or tube oils. The names of the FolkArt Artists' Pigment colors will be the same as the names of the colors in these other mediums. You should note that you can paint with tube oils on top of acrylic base coats but you cannot paint acrylic on top of tube oils.

FolkArt Artists' Pigment Acrylic Paint

These bottle acrylics are artist-grade paints with a creamy consistency much like tube oils. They are available in forty-six colors. The advantage of using these paints is that they are pure, standard colors with basic names used throughout the art world. The names are the same in tube oils, watercolor, gouache, casein, tube acrylic and some other brands of bottle acrylics. If you desire a brighter, radiant look to your painting, you will need a pure color. Other brands and lines of bottle acrylics are premixed, which

does save some time and knowledge but you will find you accumulate numerous bottles. The rewards of learning to mix your own colors will be a maturing experience in your artistic development.

I would suggest you start with a limited number of colors such as

- Alizarin Crimson
- Brilliant Ultramarine
- Burnt Umber
- Cobalt Blue
- Dioxazine Purple
- Medium Yellow
- Pure Black
- Pure Orange
- Red Light
- Titanium White

Additional colors used in this book and that are nice to have are

- Napthol Crimson
- Prussian Blue
- Raw Sienna
- Yellow Light
- Yellow Ochre

For instructions on how to mix paints, see page 15 in chapter two, Getting Started.

Brushes

The quality of the brush you paint with is very important. A good brushstroke cannot be made unless the brush bristles bend easily, then readily return to their original shape. Most brush companies offer several lines of brushes, and the old adage "you get what you pay for" prevails. Bristles can be either synthetic or animal hair. Good quality synthetic brushes are an acceptable economical substitute for animal hair. Always use the largest size brush you can within the area being painted. This will eliminate excess brushstrokes and will yield a softer appearance. Many brushes are designed specifically for certain techniques. Great artwork can be accomplished with a limited set of brushes as long as the selection is guided and deliberate. Following are the brushes I recommend you have on hand for painting the projects in this book.

Bette Byrd Brushes
- Series 400 nos. 1/0, 2/0 and 6/0 liner brushes
- Series 100 no. 1 round brush
- Series 200 nos. 2, 4, 6, 10 and 20 flat brushes
- Series 310 no. 6 bristle fan brush
- Series 510 ½-inch (12mm) mop brush
- Series 800 1-inch (25mm) flat wash brush

Plaid Brushes
- 1-inch (25mm) Poly-Sponge brush

Flat Brush. Flat brushes are traditionally used for "flat" painting such as basecoating or just filling in areas. They are also used for blending (see sidebar on page 16). For the projects in this book, flat brushes are also used to paint rounded flower petals—this avoids the stiff look of a strokework petal painted with a round brush.

Flat Wash Brush. Use the flat wash brush to basecoat and to fill in large areas of your painting. The long fibers hold a great deal of paint.

Round Brush. Round brushes are used to make fine lines for stems or veins or for outlining. They can also be used for painting dots and comma strokes. When painting linework with the round brush, thin the paint to the consistency of ink. When executing strokework, thin the paint to the consistency of nail polish. Load your brush well until all hairs are wet, but avoid filling the brush up to the ferrule (metal part).

Liner Brush. Liner brushes are long, round, thin and pointed. Use liners to make very fine lines with paint that is thinned with water.

Mop Brush. After blending colors with a flat brush, use the mop brush to eliminate brushstrokes for a soft, blended effect. Keep your mop brushes dry for blending and only dampen to clean.

Fan Brush. This brush is in the shape of a fan with hairs that separate. Use of this brush will produce separated streaks that can work well for grass or animal fur. The fan is also a great blender to soften, but not eliminate, brushstrokes.

Foam Brush. Use a foam brush (sometimes referred to as a sponge brush) for basecoating large areas. This brush has a foam sponge head on a stick handle.

For information on caring for your brushes, see page 16 in chapter two, Getting Started.

General Supplies

Following are other items I have on-hand each time I paint.

- Designs From the Heart Wood Sealer: to seal wood before painting.
- Sandpaper, 400-grit: use to sand wood pieces before painting and between layers of base coat.
- Tack cloth: for cleaning off sanding dust.
- Tracing paper: to trace patterns for transfer.
- Stylus: to trace patterns onto the painting surface.
- Black, gray and white transfer paper: for transferring patterns to pieces to be painted.
- Masterson's Sta-Wet Palette: to store puddles of paint used in a project. This plastic palette box measures 11½" x 12½" (29.2cm x 31.8cm) and is 1-inch (2.5cm) deep. The tight-fitting lid is quite easy to open and close. The palette comes equipped with a thin sponge and palette paper to keep your acrylics from drying out. See page 15 for instructions on setting up your palette.
- Scotch Brand Transparent Tape: for masking off areas when painting.
- Ruler: to measure borders.
- T-square: to draw perpendicular lines or to "square things up." In project nine, Wildflowers, the T-square is used to make sure the vertical center of the vase is parallel to the sides of the canvas and perpendicular to the bottom edge of the canvas.

- Compass: to draw circles and to measure borders on circular surfaces.
- Scissors: for cutting paper for patterns.
- FolkArt Blending Gel Medium 867: to mix with paints to add transparency or to moisten surfaces prior to painting. Blending gel medium increases the open time of acrylic paint while maintaining paint thickness. Using blending gel allows for blending colors, shading and highlighting.
- Palette knife: a tool for mixing paint on your palette.
- Small plastic container: to save left-over mixed paint.
- Spray bottle: to dampen palette as paint dries and can be used for some background techniques.
- Paper towels: for cleanup and for wiping your brush when blending.
- Brush basin: to rinse brushes with water.
- Brush Plus brush cleaner from Plaid: to thoroughly clean brushes (see Caring for Your Brushes on page 16).
- Kneaded eraser: to remove excess graphite from traced pattern.
- FolkArt Clearcote Matte Finish Acrylic Spray Sealer: to use as a finish coat on wood pieces.
- FolkArt Artists' Varnish: brushes on in thin layers for easy control. It dries clear and is non-yellowing. It's available in gloss, satin and matte finishes. Use for canvas painting.

Painting Surfaces

A variety of wood pieces and canvas has been used as painting surfaces for the projects in this book. However, don't feel limited by these items. You can find other suitable items at craft stores or wood shops in your area. You can adapt the pattern to a different piece by enlarging or reducing the pattern on a copy machine. See page 14 in chapter two, Getting Started, for more information on preparing your surface.

getting started

Preparing the Surface

Wood

Seal a wood surface with Designs From The Heart Wood Sealer. Wait one hour and sand the surface with 400-grit sandpaper, sanding with the grain of the wood. Wipe off any sanding dust with a tack cloth. Paint or stain the surface according to the directions listed with each project.

Canvas

Most purchased stretched canvas has already been primed with a sealer such as gesso. It is therefore ready to be basecoated with acrylic paints as instructed in the directions for that project.

Transferring the Pattern

Trace the pattern from the book onto tracing paper. Enlarge or reduce this pattern with the aid of a copy machine to fit the project you choose for your painting surface. Tape the pattern in place, then slip transfer paper shiny side down between the traced design and the painting surface. Trace over the lines of the pattern using a stylus. If you place a sheet of waxed paper on top of the pattern and trace with the stylus, the scratched markings will show you which lines you have traced. If the traced pattern lines are too heavy, remove some of the tracing with a kneaded eraser.

Setting Up Your Work Area

Set up your work area with your prepared project to be painted in front of you on a table or easel. Set out your paper towels, brushes, palette knife and water basin. Place your palette to either the immediate right or left of the project depending on whether you are right- or left-handed. Dip the palette sponge in water and wring it out to remove a little of the water. Soak the palette paper in water for a few minutes and place this on top of the palette sponge. Squeeze out a fifty-cent-coin-size puddle of each of the colors listed in the instructions. Place these along one side of your palette. Add an extra amount of white as that always comes in handy. Arrange the colors in the same order every time so their placement will become familiar to you. If you wish, you could place the paints following the colors on the color wheel (see page 18 for information on the color wheel).

Transfer the pattern onto the prepared surface with transfer paper and a stylus. If the pattern lines are too dark, lighten the lines with a kneaded eraser.

Place your paints on the palette keeping the bottle colors along one side and the mixes down the other. To help keep your main palette clean, you may want to mix the paint mixtures on a separate piece of palette paper and then transfer them to your main palette with your palette knife.

Preparing the Paint Mixtures

Each project in this book includes swatches of paint mixtures and the formula for mixing them. You may want to mix your paints on a separate sheet of palette paper. The paint seems to spread while mixing and will take up too much space on the palette. You then can transfer it to your painting palette.

When mixing a formula, place the amount of each of the colors listed on the palette paper and mix them together with your palette knife. Press with your knife and then scrape and press again until the colors are thoroughly mixed. Adjust colors to match the color swatch in the instructions. Remember that acrylic paints are darker when dry than when wet. You

should let a small sample dry to be sure of the match. Notice how the colors change as the mixing takes place. If you are mixing complementary colors, a softening occurs.

It is best to mix more paint than you think you will need. It is difficult to remix and match a color exactly, and it is frustrating to run out in the middle of the painting. If you are going to need a large quantity, place the mixed paint in small plastic containers with tight lids for use at a later time.

Tip

If you take a break from painting, merely snap the lid on the Sta-Wet Palette and the paints will stay wet for days. If they begin to dry out some, spray a light mist of water over them. Keep the palette level because water and paint can leak through the edge if it is tipped at an angle.

Advantages of Color Mixing

1. You are ready to paint any project without time and trouble spent finding and buying missing colors.

2. You can mix any color with only a few bottles of basic paint.

3. You will not need to pack and carry so many bottles when you travel.

4. You can substitute a different medium because oil, watercolor and other mediums have the same basic names for pure pigments.

5. You will have a better understanding of how the color was achieved.

6. You will understand color intensity and value as you experience the change from a bright pure color to a more pleasing one with softer intensity and value.

7. You will be rewarded with a maturing experience in your artistic development.

To blend colors use a flat brush that is just damp. Start with short choppy strokes and finish with long straight strokes with a light touch. Wipe the brush often on a dry rag or paper towel to eliminate excess paint.

When you're satisfied with the color, pick up the paint mix with your palette knife and transfer it to your clean palette. Write the mix number from the instructions beside each mixture on the palette paper. In the steps, the mixes are referred to by number.

In addition to mixing colors from the formulas, you can brush-mix colors when a small amount of paint is needed. To brush-mix, dip your brush into one color and then the next and stroke on the palette to mix the colors in the brush. Then apply the color to the painting. Study project one, White Poppies, for brush and blending techniques.

Color mixing can be a little intimidating, but a basic understanding of color and why certain colors are chosen will help. To help develop knowledge of color and skills at color mixing see chapter three, Color Basics.

If you prefer not to mix colors, you can use the swatches of the mixed colors to match to other bottles of premixed acrylics.

Caring for Your Brushes

Before picking up paint with a brush, dip the brush in water and dry on a towel. If the paint is stiff, dip the corner of the brush in water or blending gel and then into the paint. Work the paint and water together some on your palette before you begin painting.

As you're painting these projects, clean your brush between colors with water only when making a drastic color change such as from white to black. Otherwise, merely wipe your brush on a paper towel before switching to the next color.

Treat your brush with care and don't scrub it on the paper towel.

Cleaning your brushes thoroughly after each painting session is extremely important. A brush can be ruined after only one use if paint is left to dry in the bristles. Rinse the bristles in water after using acrylic paints or watercolors. Rinse the bristles in paint thinner after using tube oils. After rinsing, work in a good brush cleaner, such as Brush Plus from Plaid. Then wash the bristles with mild soap and water. Rinse again and shape the wet bristles to a flat or pointed shape. Place the brush in a location where the hairs are not touching anything and allow to dry. If the bristles becomes unruly, run the clean bristles over a bar of mild soap. Let the soap dry to shape bristles. Before painting again, rinse brush with water for acrylics or watercolor or paint thinner for oils.

Drying and Finishing

Acrylic paints dry rapidly. To speed up the drying process even more, you can use a blow hair dryer.

After the paint has dried, remove any pattern lines that may still be visible with a paper towel dampened with water.

When the painting is complete, you will want to add a finish coat to your project to protect and add richness to the color. For the wood pieces, use two coats of FolkArt Clearcote Matte Finish Acrylic Spray Sealer. For the canvas, use FolkArt Artists' Varnish satin finish.

1. Use the largest brushes you can handle in any given area. This will seem clumsy but will make it nearly impossible to paint in a detailed style.

2. Paint many of the details with the corner of a flat brush instead of a round brush. This will give you irregular shapes.

3. Hold the brush well back on the handle as you paint. This too will keep you from painting each exact minute part. Work for a light, easy touch.

4. Use a slip-slap method of blending. After laying on the colors, use a damp flat brush to blend colors together, making short choppy (but straight) strokes in all directions. Wipe the brush on a paper towel often as you blend.

5. Use the pattern design as a general composition, but purposely paint outside the outline. Forget about coloring books and crayons. Trace your pattern on lightly so it will not be difficult to cover the lines. Feel free to change anything you like so it will be your own idea.

6. Leave the painting in a somewhat unfinished state with little blending. Make yourself stop before you think the painting is finished.

7. Keep the outer edges of leaves and flowers softened. Avoid as many hard edges as possible.

8. Don't include every detail, only enough to give the effect. Your painting will look overworked if you add all the small details you'd find in a realistic painting.

9. Back away from your painting often as you paint. The painting should look better from a distance than up close.

10. Take off your glasses or squint and look at your painting up close. This will give the same effect as backing away.

11. Paint fast, as if you are in a hurry to get finished.

12. Don't fiddle with the painting. Avoid reworking. You might be surprised at the end results and realize that each spot does not need to be perfect.

13. Let yourself go. Don't worry what others will think or how the painting will look in your house.

14. Paint with thinned, transparent paint. Several layers of transparent paint will produce a softening result in your painting.

15. Exaggerate colors boldly. If you see a little red in a flower, make it brighter in your painting.

16. Keep saying, "My painting will not look exactly like this painted sample." This is your painting and the sample is given only as an idea.

color basics

The color swatches of each paint mixture used are given with each project's instructions in this book. Some notes are also given regarding the reason for the mixtures. In hopes that you will develop a better understanding of how to mix your own colors, you will first need to learn some basic color theory. A system of mixing can be learned which is quite simple. However, like so many "simple" things, it requires some study and practice. Start from the beginning and learn each step thoroughly as you proceed. Your other option is just to buy more bottles of premixed paint, which would be more pleasing than pure colors. With the added expense and extra storage of additional paints, however, you probably will want to mix colors.

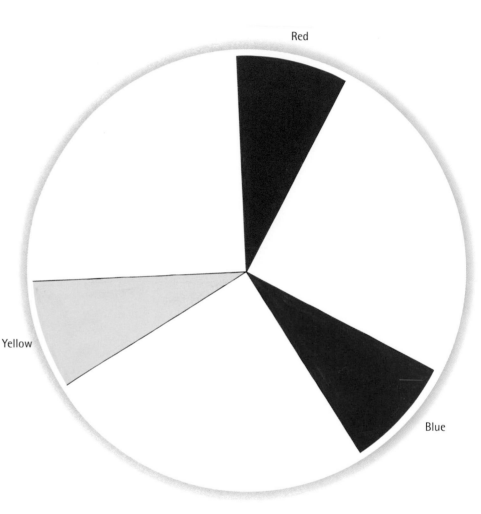

The Color Wheel

Use the color wheels on these pages for reference when using the Folk-Art Artists' Pigment acrylics. Or better yet, make your own color wheel. Much is to be learned by experiencing the mixing yourself. Trace the color wheel patterns from this book and paint the color wheel following the procedure given. You will need these paint colors to create your own color wheel:

Alizarin Crimson
Cobalt Blue
Dioxazine Purple
Medium Yellow
Pure Orange
Red Light

Primary Colors

Red, yellow and blue are the primary colors and cannot be mixed from any other colors. In making your own color wheel, use a limited number of colors to more easily understand their mixing. Use Red Light + Alizarin Crimson in the red space, Medium Yellow in the yellow space, and Cobalt Blue in the blue space.

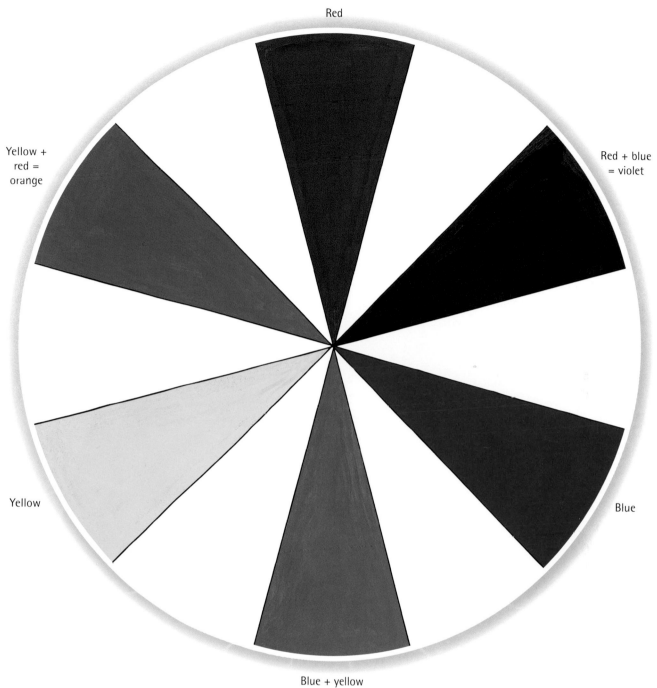

Red

Red + blue = violet

Yellow + red = orange

Blue

Yellow

Blue + yellow = green

Secondary Colors

Orange, green and violet are the secondary colors. Theoretically, this set of colors can be produced by mixing together two of the primaries: red + yellow = orange; yellow + blue = green; and red + blue = violet. However, in some cases pure color is difficult to mix.

Violet, for instance, can be impossible to mix from pure red and pure blue if the red pigment contains a bit of orange. The problem arises when that bit of orange mixes with the pure blue. Orange and blue are complementary, and when they are mixed the result is a dull, muddy color. When red that contains a bit of orange is mixed with blue, the result is a dull, muddy purple.

If you make your own color wheel, use Dioxazine Purple FolkArt Artists' Pigment acrylic in the violet space for a bright, clean color.

For the rest of the secondary colors, use Pure Orange in the orange space and a mixture of Cobalt Blue + Medium Yellow in the green space.

Intermediate Colors

The intermediate, or tertiary, colors result from mixing a primary color with a secondary color. For example, yellow, a primary color, is mixed with orange, a secondary color, to create the intermediate color yellow-orange. When stating an intermediate color, the name of the primary color always comes first.

In your color wheel use Alizarin Crimson in the red-violet space, again because a bit of orange in the pure red pigment may make your red-violet too muddy. But mix all the rest of the intermediate colors using the primary and secondary colors.

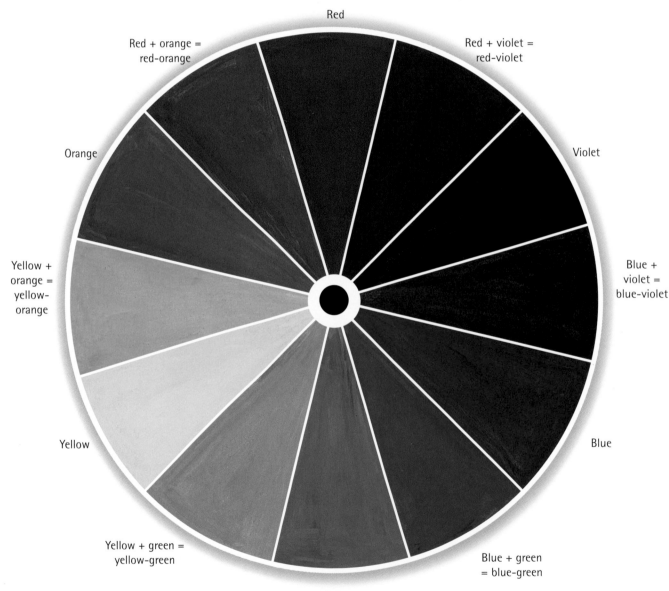

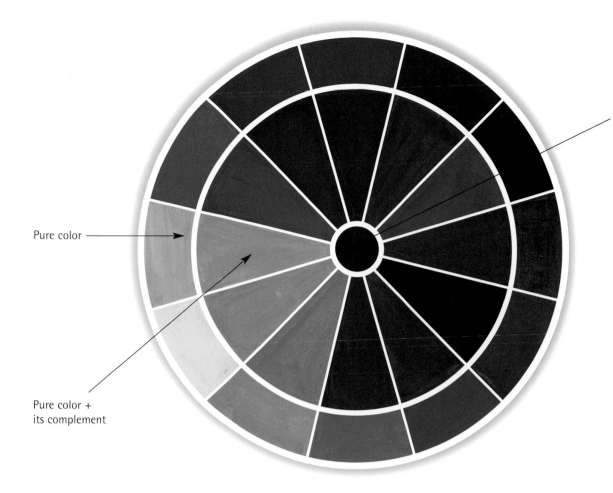

The center circle is a mix of equal amounts of any two colors opposite each other on the color wheel. The resulting color will be some variety of muddy brown.

Pure color

Pure color + its complement

Color Intensity

Think about creating a center of interest in your painting—it is done through design and color. One area in a design is intended to be the center of interest, but the colors used in that area will truly make it stand apart from the rest of the painting. The intensity of the colors used can help to establish the center of interest. Intensity refers to the brightness or dullness of a color. If your design is a vase of flowers with a strong light source, then use your intense colors where the light shines on the flowers that are the center of interest. Use less intense, or dull, colors on the secondary flowers and leaves so that they stay in the background.

The full color wheel above shows how you can change the intensity of a color to fit its place in the design. The outer spaces of this color wheel are the basic, or pure, colors discussed previously. The inner spaces show each color changed by adding its complementary color. The complementary color is the color that lies opposite a color on the color wheel. The complement of red, for example, is green; the complement of orange is blue; the complement of yellow is violet. If you add a small amount of the complementary color to a pure color the result is a duller, less intense color. As you are painting and your color seems too bright, you now know that you can add the color's complement to dull the color and make it less bright.

If your color wheel isn't nearby while you're painting, you can keep in mind the fact that the complement of the three primary colors is a mixture of the other two primaries. So, the complement of yellow is blue + red (which is violet); the complement of blue is red + yellow (orange); and the complement of red is blue + yellow (green).

There are other ways to change the intensity of a color. You can add an earth color, such as burnt umber, raw umber, raw sienna or yellow ochre. Also you can add black to a color for this same purpose.

Color Value

The value of a color refers to the lightness or darkness of the color. In painting, you need to understand value in order to give form and shape to objects such as flowers, stems and leaves. An object is lightest in the spot where the light shines directly on the object at a 90° angle (this is where you'd place a highlight value). As the object turns away from the light, the value gradually darkens. In the shadows, where there is an absence of light, a very dark value is needed.

A good example of this is in the painting of the hibiscus in project four. It is obvious where the light is shining and where it is shadowed. Not only do the leaves have a light value but also a reflected bright highlight is created giving the leaves their shiny appearance. A definite center of interest is formed by placing the lightest values in the upper left center of the painting. This is where we see the most contrast between dark and light values—your eye is drawn to this point.

Notice that even the stems and branches are given shape and dimension through the placement of light and dark values.

To lighten a color's value, add white or some other light color. To darken a color's value, add black or some other dark color. A light color is said to have a high value; a dark color has a low value.

Notice how the values used to paint this project give the flowers, leaves and stems shape and dimension. Instructions for painting this project begin on page 60.

A Study in Intensity and Value

To illustrate this color information, let's consider some roses, similar to those in project nine. To paint the roses, I have selected three bottled colors: Titanium White, Red Light and Thicket. From these colors, I have created a value scale—ranging from Titanium White to Red Light—and an intensity scale—from Red Light + Titanium White to Thicket.

The value scale shows a range of pinks to use to paint the roses. The lightest values are placed more on the flower that is to be the center of interest. The darker values are placed in shadow areas and on the background flower.

The intensity scale shows colors that could be used to change the intensity of the flowers. The more intense colors (those on the left end of the scale) can be used to shade the flower in the center of interest. The colors toward the middle of the scale can be used to shade the background flower.

To paint the flowers on the right, I didn't use all the colors in the scales, but you can see that a number of different values and intensities were used. When you mix your own colors, it's easier to get a range of values and intensities than it would be if you didn't mix and used only pre-mixed bottled paints.

Titanium White   Red Light   Thicket

Value Scale

Titanium
White   Red Light

Intensity Scale

Red Light +   Thicket
Titanium White

The flower on the left was painted with colors that have a high value and a high intensity. This combination makes the flower very eye-catching and is therefore good for a flower in the center of interest. The flower to the right was painted with colors of a lower value and lower intensity. It works well in the background and serves as a contrast to the lighter, brighter flower.

white poppies

This project is a great lesson in learning the basics of loosening up your painting style. If you will practice this lesson first, you will then understand the different strokes referred to throughout this book.

This project is also a great lesson in color. A very limited palette has been used—a total of only five bottles of acrylic paint. The color scheme of the project is primarily monochromatic—blue and white, with orange added to dull the blue. Orange is the complementary color of blue and will, therefore, change blue's intensity when they are mixed together. You will notice when you mix your palette colors how bright the Cobalt Blue mixed with the Warm White becomes. But as you begin to add small amounts of Pure Orange to this mixture, the intensity of the blue will lessen and the resulting color will be very soft.

Materials

Paint: (FA) = FolkArt Acrylics; (AP) = FolkArt Artists' Pigment Acrylics

402 Light Blue (FA)

420 Linen (FA)

720 Cobalt Blue (AP)

628 Pure Orange (AP)

988 Warm White (FA)

Mix 1: Light Blue + Linen (2:1)

Mix 2: Warm White + Cobalt Blue + Pure Orange (4:1:1)

Mix 3: Warm White + Cobalt Blue + Pure Orange (4:2:1)

Mix 4: Cobalt Blue + Pure Orange (3:1)

Brushes
- no. 2/0 liner
- no. 1 round
- no. 6 flat or ¼" (6mm) flat
- no. 10 flat or ⅜" (10mm) flat
- no. 20 flat or ½" (12mm) flat
- 1" (25mm) foam

Additional Supplies
- 867 FolkArt Blending Gel Medium

Surface
- 11" x 13" (28cm x 33cm) wooden plaque from Hofcraft

This pattern may
be hand-traced or
photocopied for
personal use only.
Enlarge at 161
percent to bring
up to full size.

Preparation and Background

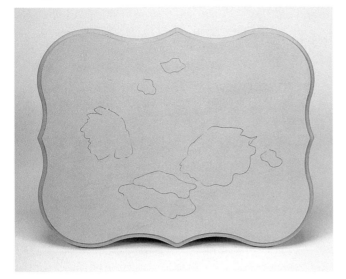

1 | Seal the entire surface with wood sealer. Sand when dry with fine sandpaper and wipe off dust with a tack cloth. Basecoat the board with mix 1 and the 1" (25mm) foam brush until well covered. Transfer the pattern for just the main flowers onto the surface with dark transfer paper. If the lines appear too dark, wipe over them with a kneaded eraser to remove some of the graphite and lighten them because heavy lines could be difficult to cover with paint. This pattern will be obscured during the background painting, but it will help to gauge where to place the light and dark values. After the background has dried, you can then retrace your pattern if you wish.

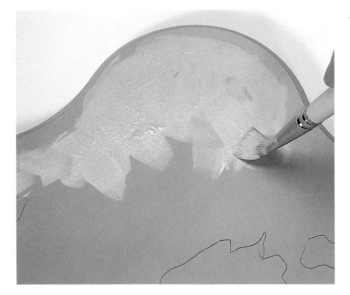

2 | With a no. 20 flat brush, pick up mix 1, blending gel and a little water and work this into the brush on the palette. Brush this mixture around the edge of the flowers, pulling the paint onto the flowers some.

3 | Load mix 2, blending gel and a little water on the no. 20 flat brush and work into the brush on the palette. Paint this mix with slip-slap strokes next to the flowers, leaving the lighter value toward the edge of the board.

Slip-slap Brushstroke for Blending

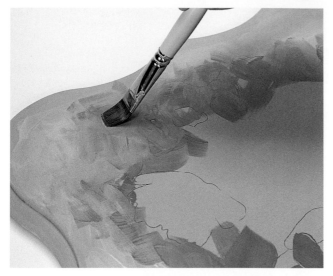

4 Rinse the brush and blot on a towel. Blend the colors together where they meet with slip-slap brushstrokes. Work the brush in short choppy, but straight, strokes in all directions. Wipe the brush often on a paper towel as you work to remove the paint. The resulting background should be soft and blotchy.

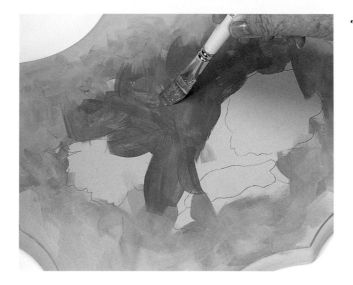

5 Rinse the brush and load with mix 3, blending gel and water. Work the mix into the brush on the palette. Slip-slap this mixture between the flowers in the center of the piece. Again, disregard the pattern and paint onto the flowers.

6 Continue working the background, picking up additional paint if necessary, until you get a nice gradation of color from light on the outside to dark toward the center.

Slip-slide Brushstroke to Paint Leaves

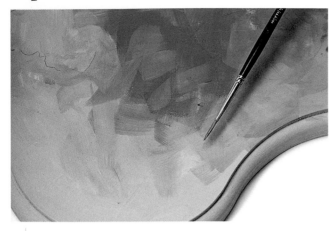

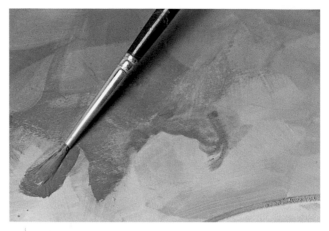

7 | Load mix 3 on the no. 2/0 liner brush with lots of water and blending gel. The paint should be the consistency of thin nail polish. Hold the brush loosely at the back end of the handle and place the bristles parallel to the surface.

8 | Press the brush on the surface.

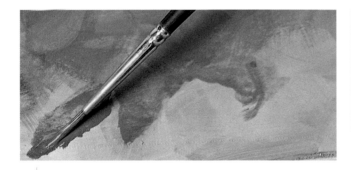

9 | With a light touch, slip and slide the brush as you lift it slightly. Push away from yourself or pull toward yourself only the short distance of a leaf. This will give you an irregular shape that might not resemble the shape of a leaf.

10 | Slide the brush and lift it off the surface.

11 | Continue making these slip-slide strokes using mixes 1, 2 and 3. For contrast, place some lighter-colored leaves in the dark areas and darker-colored leaves in the light areas.

Sweeping Brushstroke to Paint Leaves

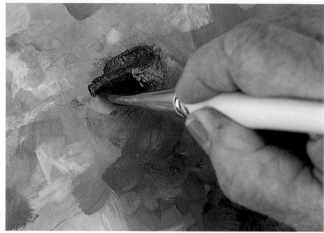

12 For slightly larger leaves, load the no. 20 flat brush with mix 4 and blending gel. Work the paint into the brush on the palette. Hold the brush so the handle is at a 45° angle to the surface, with the handle pointed back toward you. Press the corner of the brush down onto the surface so the bristles spread, bending the bristles either to the right or left.

13 Pull the brush only a short distance, lifting the brush as you move from right to left or from left to right. The movement will be similar to sweeping with a small broom. Do not turn the brush. The result is a loosely formed leaf. Some strokes may be partial and incomplete leaves. Some may be somewhat ragged in appearance, and these you may want to overstroke with a rinsed and wiped brush. But stop adjusting the leaves before you think they are really finished.

14 Fill in the center of the surface with these loose, dark leaves. This area should be especially dark to contrast with the white flowers. Continue to paint these leaves using all the mixes used so far.

15 Let the leaves dry completely, then transfer the complete pattern to the surface with white transfer paper and a stylus. If needed, use dark transfer paper over the light background areas. If the pattern lines are too heavy, go over them with a kneaded eraser to remove some of the graphite.

Thin Line Strokes to Paint Stems and Veins

16 To paint stems for this project (and veins in leaves for other projects), load a no. 2/0 or finer liner brush with mix 3 paint thinned with water only. (The water will allow the paint to flow better than blending gel.) The paint should be as thin as ink. Fill the entire brush with paint, but avoid getting paint up into the metal ferrule. Work the paint into the bristles on the palette.

For the long stems in this project, hold the brush back on the tip of the handle and paint with long loose strokes. No part of your hand or arm will be resting on the surface. Press the brush slightly to widen the stroke or lift to narrow the stroke.

17 Pull long thin lines for the background stems with mixes 1, 2 and 4. Paint light stems in the dark areas and dark stems in the light outer areas.

To use this technique for short lines in other projects, hold the brush close to the bristles as you would when writing with a pencil. Rest the weight of your painting hand in your other hand. Hold the little finger of the painting hand straight and touch it to the surface—the remainder of your hand and arm is off the surface. This position gives you freedom to swing the brush in a graceful arch.

Small Petal or Leaf Stroke

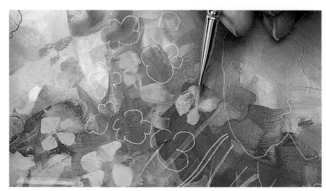

18 Paint small blossoms around the pattern blossoms using the same sweeping stroke as in steps 12 and 13, but use the smaller no. 6 flat instead of the larger no. 20 flat. Load the no. 6 flat brush with mix 3 and a bit of water. Pull the brush from the outside of the petal into the center, lifting the brush only slightly. Pull the stroke only a very short distance to make a short rounded petal-type stroke.

19 Paint blossoms in and around the pattern-traced blossoms first, continuing with mix 3. Then paint lighter blossoms using mix 2. Let some of the strokes overlap, and let some of the blossoms be incomplete. Remember, these blossoms are painted around the pattern blossoms.

Small Petals, continued

20 | Using the same brush and technique, fill in the blossoms from the pattern with mix 1.

21 | Highlight a few of the pattern petals by painting over them with Warm White loaded on the no. 6 flat.

Large Petal or Leaf Strokes for Painting the Poppies

22 | Paint the poppies using the sweeping stroke from steps 12 and 13, but use the midsized no. 10 flat brush. Load the brush with Warm White, and place the corner of the flat brush on the surface at the outer edge of the poppy petal, slightly past the pattern line. Press the brush onto the surface so the bristles bend.

23 | Lift the brush slightly and sweep the brush toward the center of the flower.

24 | Lift the brush at the end of the stroke.

25   Basecoat each poppy with this stroke, laying the strokes on so they fan out from the center of the flower. Paint the underneath petal of each flower first. For good coverage, paint each flower with three coats of Warm White, using the sweeping stroke for all the coats.

26   Load the no. 10 flat brush with a mixture of mix 1 + mix 2 (1:1). Overstroke the inner parts of the underneath petals using the same sweeping stroke. Paint a little of this color on the backsides of the top petals as well. Load the brush with mix 3 and overstroke the small dark areas where one petal overlaps another, this time working from the center toward the outer edge.

Glazing

Outlining

27   Glazing can be used to soften any part of the painting and eliminate a harsh look or to change a color. To make a glaze, mix a very small amount of paint, usually a medium value, with water or blending gel so that it is barely colored. Paint over the dry surface to lighten, darken or add a tint of color to a section.

In this project, soften the harshness of the shadows on the petals by glazing over the blossoms with a thin wash of Warm White using the no. 10 flat.

28   Using the no. 1 round brush, outline the petals with Warm White, keeping the strokes loose and random. The strokes should simulate the wavy edges of the poppy.

Flower Centers

29 | Load the no. 1 round brush with mix 4 and tap in the stamen dots on the two right-hand flowers.

30 | Rinse the brush and load with Warm White. Paint in dots in the centers of the two right-hand poppies. Add a few dots near the clusters of white fill-flowers and in the lower left corner of the pattern.

31 | Add the center to the small fill-flowers with the mix 4 on the no. 1 round. Tap in just a few dots to make these flowers complete. Leave some flowers without centers.

Buds

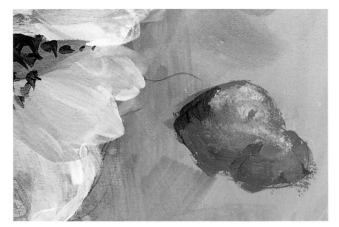

32 | Load the no. 10 flat brush with a mixture of mix 2 + mix 3 and fill in the buds. Shade the buds with mix 4 and highlight with Warm White.

Stems

33 | Load the no. 1 round with a mixture of mix 1 + Warm White. Paint in the three main stems on the left side of the piece. Use mix 4 for the stem on the right-hand bud.

34 | Create the effect of fuzz on the stems and buds with tiny dots of thinned mix 1 on the no. 1 round brush.

35 | To suggest the presence of more leaves, load the no. 1 round brush with very thin mix 2 and outline some background shapes to resemble leaves. These can be done at random throughout the design.

Border

36 Using the no. 10 flat brush and mix 3 thinned with blending gel, run the brush along the crease on the edge of the board.

37 With a paper towel, wipe off any paint that has gotten on the sides of the surface, leaving the paint in the crease only.

38 | Varnish with two coats of FolkArt Matte Finish Acrylic Sealer spray.

pansies

After studying the white poppies project, this is a good first piece to choose because it uses the same techniques you have practiced and the pattern is uncomplicated in size and number of flowers.

You will notice that again I've used complementary colors to achieve a softer, duller intensity of yellow and purple mixes. Mix 6, a purple, includes orange, which has yellow in it, and mix 7, a yellow, includes purple. Yellow and purple are complementary colors, which lie opposite each other on the color wheel.

Materials

Paint: (FA) = FolkArt Acrylics; (AP) = FolkArt Artists' Pigment Acrylics

420 Linen (FA) | 480 Titanium White (AP) | 918 Yellow Light (AP) | 628 Pure Orange (AP)

629 Red Light (AP) | 484 Brilliant Ultramarine (AP) | 463 Dioxazine Purple (AP) | 479 Pure Black (AP)

Mix 1: Brilliant Ultramarine + Pure Black + Yellow Light (1:2:2)

Mix 2: Yellow Light + Pure Black + Brilliant Ultramarine (3:1:1)

Mix 3: Yellow Light + Titanium White + Pure Black + Brilliant Ultramarine (3:2:1:1)

Mix 4: Yellow Light + Titanium White (1:1)

Mix 5: Titanium White + Brilliant Ultramarine (3:1)

Mix 6: Brilliant Ultramarine + Dioxazine Purple + Titanium White + Pure Orange (2:1:3:1)

Mix 7: Yellow Light + Dioxazine Purple (4:1)

Mix 8: Yellow Light + Pure Orange (3:1)

Mix 9: Red Light + Dioxazine Purple (1:1)

Mix 10: Pure Black + Dioxazine Purple (1:1)

Brushes
- no. 1 liner
- no. 1 round
- no. 4 flat or ⅛" (3mm) flat
- no. 6 flat or ¼" (6mm) flat
- no. 20 flat or ½" (12mm) flat
- old, scruffy no. 6 flat or ¼" (6mm) flat
- 1" (25mm) foam

Additional Supplies
- 867 FolkArt Blending Gel Medium

Surface
- 9" x 12" (22.9cm x 30.5cm) oval wooden plate from Walnut Hollow

These patterns may
be hand-traced or
photocopied for
personal use only.
The pattern for the
center of the plate,
left, and the pattern
for the border, right,
are shown here at
full size.

Preparation

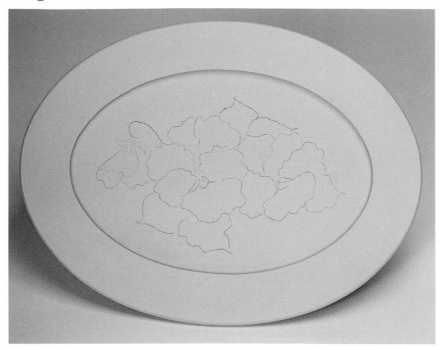

1 | Seal the entire plate with wood sealer. When dry, sand the plate with 400-grit sandpaper. Clean off the dust with a tack cloth. Basecoat the plate with Linen on the 1-inch foam brush until well covered. When dry, transfer the pattern with dark transfer paper. If your tracing lines appear too dark, wipe over the pattern lines with a kneaded eraser to remove some of the graphite. Prepare the paint mixtures listed in the materials list and place them on your palette.

Background Greenery

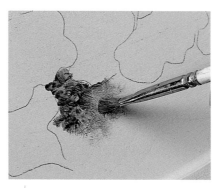

2 | Pick up some of mix 1 along with a small amount of blending gel on the no. 6 flat brush. Dab the paint on to the surface with the corner of the brush, placing it in splotchy bunches around the outer edge of the pattern.

3 | While the paint is still wet, soften the paint a bit by scrubbing it with a dry no. 6 flat brush. To avoid brush damage, use a worn, scruffy brush.

4 | Place these patches of greenery at random around the outer edges of the pattern. The greens should be a darker value adjacent to the pattern and fade to a lighter value where you have scrubbed.

Leaves

5 For variety, paint each of the leaves with different combinations of colors. Begin with the darkest value on each leaf. For the darkest leaves, use the no. 4 flat brush with mix 1. Base in the areas along the center vein and where the leaf is overlapped by another leaf, creating a cast shadow. For the lighter leaves, paint these same areas with mix 2. Pull the strokes in the direction of the veins.

6 Next, paint the medium value for the leaves. For the dark leaves, use mix 2 on the no. 4 flat and pull the strokes from the edge of the leaf in toward the center. Let dry, then paint another coat of both the dark and medium values on a dark leaf. While the paint is still wet, blend the values. Lay the no. 4 flat brush along the center of the leaf, press the brush, then pull and lift the brush, following the direction of the veins. Also blend from the edge of the leaf into the center using the same diagonal strokes. Wipe the brush on a paper towel often. Repeat this technique on all the dark leaves.

   Basecoat the medium value on the light leaves with mix 3. Let dry, then basecoat the dark and medium values of the light leaves again and blend as described above.

7 Highlight the leaves with mix 3 for the dark leaves and with mix 4 for the light leaves. Pull the strokes from the edge of the leaf onto the medium value. Two coats of paint will be necessary.

8 With mix 5, add a bit of blue to the lighter values of some of the leaves. This is a reflected cool light.

9 | Add a glaze of orange to the two lightest leaves with mix 8 (see glazing technique on page 33). Place this color on the lightest area of the light leaves.

10 | Paint the veins on the leaves with the no. 1 liner brush loaded with paint thinned with water to a fluid consistency. For the dark veins, load the brush with thinned mix 1. Paint the center vein on a leaf, then pull the smaller veins from the center as you lift your brush, decreasing the size of the vein line. Refer to the instructions for painting thin line strokes on page 31. For the light veins use mix 4, then add a few veins with mix 5.

11 | With mixes 4 and 5, randomly outline some of the edges of the leaves. Keep the lines broken and paint with a light touch to avoid a rigid appearance.

12 | To create a turned-up edge on one leaf, load the liner brush with mix 1. Following the edge of the leaf, paint a rippled line that is thick in some areas and thin in others.

Base Coat for Petals

13 Basecoat all the petals with a thin coat of Titanium White, using the very loose sweeping stroke described on page 30. With the no. 6 flat brush, start the stroke at the edge of the petal and pull into the center. Use the same brush to blend the petal strokes slightly while the paint is still wet. Wipe the brush on a paper towel as you pick up excess paint. Some of the brushstrokes should still be visible.

Yellow Petals

14 With the no. 6 flat, paint a thin coat of mix 4 on the yellow flower petals and the bud. Again use the sweeping brushstroke and pull loose strokes from the edge of the petal into the center.

15 Load mix 7 on the brush and darken the underneath petal of the bud. Fan the brushstrokes from the outer edge of the petal toward the flower center. Leave the brushstrokes underblended. On the large yellow flower, paint mix 7 on parts of all the petals, especially those in the center section, as shown.

16 Add orange tints of mix 8 to a few spots on the petals and the bud.

17 With mix 9, add a bright red tint to the center of the lower petal of the bud.

18 Highlight the lightest petals on the bud and flower with mix 4.

19 Outline some parts of the petals with the no. 1 round brush and Titanium White thinned with water to a fluid consistency. Keep the lines loose and flowing.

Tip

Refer to page 17 for more tips and techniques for a loose style of painting.

Blue Petals

20 Load the no. 6 flat brush with mix 5 and loosely basecoat the blue flower using the sweeping stroke. Again fan the bristles at the outer edge of the petal and pull the stroke toward the center of the flower, lifting the brush as you pull.

21 While the basecoat is still wet, darken the petals with mix 6. Pull this color from the center of the flower toward the outside edge of the petal. Lift the brush at the end of the stroke so the color blends into the basecoat. If the basecoat dries, add more of mix 5 to allow open time for the colors to blend. Paint the two upper petals the darkest where they are overlapped by the front petals.

22 Paint the bottom three petals with a glaze made with water and a tiny amount of mix 4.

23 Highlight some of the petals with a fairly thick amount of Titanium White. Using the no. 1 round brush, pull the strokes down into the other colors, lifting the brush at the end of the strokes. Outline some of the petals with Titanium White as shown. If the flower appears somewhat stiff and under-blended, let it dry and glaze over the flower with a little dirty paint water from your brush basin.

Flower Center

24 Base in the flower centers with mix 8 on the no. 1 round brush. Darken the inner part of each center with a bit of mix 6. Add additional white lines around the centers to help fill them in.

25 To begin the beard of the pansies, thin mix 10 with water. Paint the base of the bottom petals using the no. 1 round brush as shown on the far right petal.

26 With the no. 1 fine liner brush and mix 10, pull lines out onto the petals. Vary the length of the lines and keep them all radiating out from the center.

27 Repeat steps 25 and 26 for the bottom three petals on each flower.

Stems

Mix 2

Mix 3

Mix 1

28 With the no. 1 liner brush, paint in the stems that lay over a light area with mix 3. Paint stems running over the dark areas with mix 1. On the bud, paint the small cap leaves with mix 2.

Border

29 To keep the border design flowing naturally, it is best to paint it freehand. However, the pattern is provided if you choose to use it. To make the vine, thin mix 1 with water and load onto the no. 1 liner. Lift your arm completely off the table and paint a free-flowing line with curves and twists.

30 Load the no. 6 flat brush with the same thinned mix and paint tiny leaves using the small leaf stroke described on page 31. Place these randomly along the vine.

31 | Spray the dry finished project with one or two coats of FolkArt Matte Finish Acrylic Sealer.

white roses

*Y*ou will see many styles of gorgeous roses done by decorative painters. Those stroke roses are accomplished by many hours of practice, using the best brushes and a lot of hand and finger control. The roses in this project seem so simple compared to the beautifully controlled stroke rose. But you will find that sometimes the easiest-looking things are the most difficult to paint.

An ice skater or pianist makes her art look so easy, but you know the thought, preparation and dedication that went into it. So it is with these roses. You must be willing to let yourself go and paint with abandon. Be willing to wait for the end when everything pulls together for a lovely, soft overall appeal.

Notice that mix 2 is made from blue and orange. These colors lie opposite each other on the color wheel and will, therefore, dull or soften a color when mixed together. A lovely soft blue is the result of adding the orange to the blue.

Materials

Paint: (FA) = FolkArt Acrylics; (AP) = FolkArt Artists' Pigment Acrylics

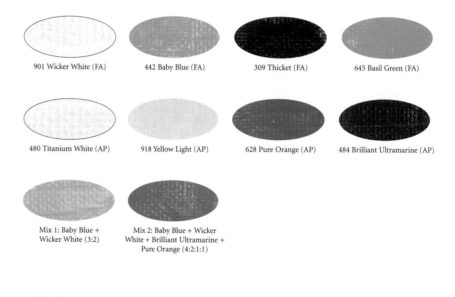

901 Wicker White (FA) 442 Baby Blue (FA) 309 Thicket (FA) 645 Basil Green (FA)

480 Titanium White (AP) 918 Yellow Light (AP) 628 Pure Orange (AP) 484 Brilliant Ultramarine (AP)

Mix 1: Baby Blue + Wicker White (3:2)

Mix 2: Baby Blue + Wicker White + Brilliant Ultramarine + Pure Orange (4:2:1:1)

Brushes

- no. 6/0 liner
- no. 1 round
- no. 4 flat or ⅛" (3mm) flat
- no. 6 flat or ¼" (6mm) flat
- no. 20 flat or ½" (12mm) flat
- 1" (25mm) foam

Additional Supplies

- 867 FolkArt Blending Gel Medium

Surface

- Wooden cake plate from Viking Woodcrafts, consisting of one plate each 14" (35.6cm) diameter and 10" (25.4cm) diameter and one center spindle 7" (17.8cm) high

This pattern may be hand-traced or photocopied for personal use only. Enlarge at 111 percent to bring it to full size. Repeat this pattern three times around the circumference of the large plate.

Preparation

1 Apply a coat of wood sealer to plates and spindle. When dry, sand until smooth. Wipe with a tack cloth. With the 1-inch (25mm) foam brush apply several coats of mix 1 to each piece until well covered, sanding between coats.

Beginning with the small plate, spread a heavy coat of blending gel on one half of the rim of the plate with the no. 20 flat.

This project calls for both Wicker White and Titanium White. They are basically the same color, but the textures and uses are very different. Wicker White is a FolkArt Acrylic color, so it is fluid and works well for basecoating and filling in brushstrokes generally. Titanium White is a FolkArt Artists' Pigment Acrylic color, so it is thicker and has a dense amount of pigment. It works well for highlighting and whenever you want the white to stand out.

Small Plate

2 With the same brush, dab mix 2 thinned with water onto the rim. Place this blue mix in loose splotches around this half of the rim.

3 Dab Baby Blue, Basil Green and Thicket on the rim in the same manner. Rinse the brush after each addition.

4 Dribble drops of water on the wet paint with the no. 20 flat brush. Add enough water to make the paint run. Any paint or water that gets in the center of the plate can be cleaned up later.

Small Plate, *continued*

5 | Add or adjust colors with your brush until you reach a soft splotchy effect. Do not blend or try to smooth out the colors.

6 | Repeat this process on the other half of the plate. Let this dry. A hair dryer will shorten the drying time, but be aware that the blowing may move the paint or water around.

7 | Paint a few stems with Thicket or Titanium White using the no. 6/0 liner brush and thinned paint. See instructions for painting thin line strokes on page 31. The painting on the small plate is now complete.

Large Plate

8 | Working on one-third of the large plate at a time, repeat the steps used for painting the small plate—start by applying the blending gel in step 1 and continue through step 6. Proceed with painting the remaining thirds of the large plate.

Transfer the pattern onto the surface with white transfer paper and a pen or stylus, repeating the pattern three times around the circumference of the plate. To achieve a very soft effect, it's best to trace only an oval for the roses and paint the petals in freehand. Each person's roses will be unique. For this photo the pattern was outlined with a liner brush and white paint.

Roses

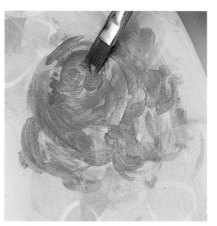

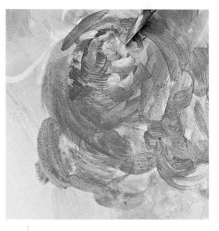

9 | Loosely paint in the oval shape of the roses with mix 2 and blending gel on a no. 6 flat brush. Follow the curve of the oval letting the brushstrokes show without blending.

10 | Dab Pure Orange in the center of the rose with the same brush.

11 | While the paint is still wet, dab Yellow Light into the center.

Roses, *continued*

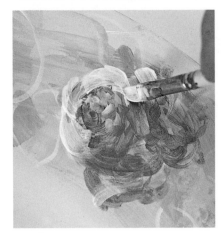

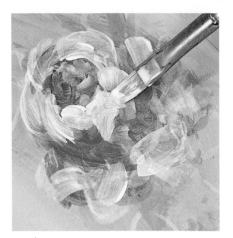

12 | Holding the no. 6 flat brush near the handle end, paint loose petal strokes with Titanium White and blending gel. Start by making the strokes around the top outer edge.

13 | Before beginning the lower petals, notice their shape in the image above. With quite a bit of Titanium White on the no. 6 flat brush, lay the brush on the surface and slide it along. Don't fiddle with the strokes.

14 | Next paint in the strokes just below the flower center.

15 | Form the bowl of the rose with long strokes that follow the curves of the rose.

16 | Paint a few thin line-stroked petals with the no. 1 round brush and Titanium White.

17 | With the no. 1 round brush, tap a few dots of mix 2 and Yellow Light into the center of the rose.

Tip

Refer to page 17 for more tips and techniques for a loose style of painting.

18 Paint each rose in this manner, turning the roses slightly so that each rose in a grouping of three faces in a different direction.

Buds

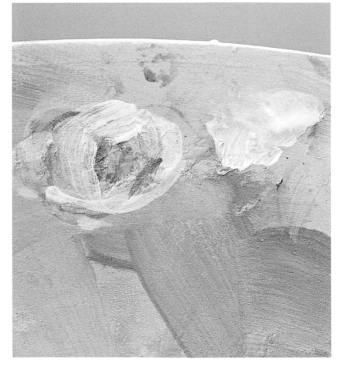

19 The bud at the end of each grouping of three roses is painted similarly to the roses. First rough in the shape with mix 2 on the no. 4 flat brush. Then tap in the center with Pure Orange and Yellow Light. Add strokes of Titanium White with the no. 4 flat, following the curves of the buds.

Leaves

20 With mix 2 on the no. 6 flat, paint loosely formed leaves around the flowers using the sweeping stroke described on page 30.

21 Dab some Basil Green leaves around the branches and buds with the no. 6 flat. Highlight some of these leaves with thinned Yellow Light.

Leaves, continued

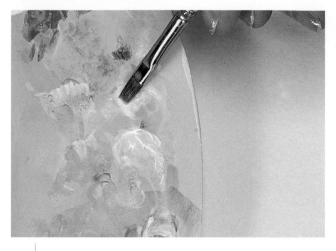

22 Highlight some of the leaves further with Titanium White.

23 Overstroke the large leaves between the roses with thinned Thicket on the no. 6 flat brush. Again use the loose, sweeping stroke to paint the leaves.

Branches

24 Paint the main branches with thinned Thicket on the no. 1 round brush. With thinned Thicket on the liner brush, paint the fine branches, small stems, thorns, leaflets around the buds and outlines on a few leaves.

Spindle

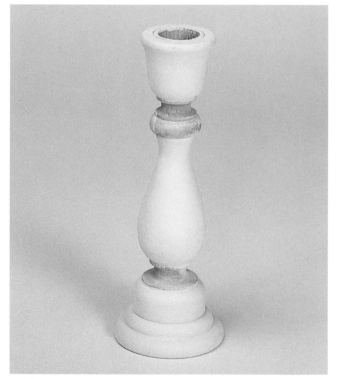

25 Paint the small shaped parts of the spindle with Pure Orange. When dry, thin mix 1 and glaze it over the Pure Orange.

26 Spray all the pieces with two coats of FolkArt Matte Finish Acrylic Sealer. Then attach the pieces with screws.

hibiscus

The brilliance of these flowers is accomplished by two methods. The first is basecoating the flowers with white and then painting over them with red. The red is somewhat transparent and the white shines through. The second method is using a complementary color scheme of red and green. The bright red flowers against the dark green background is a lively contrast of color. If the background had been brown, for instance, the red would not seem so brilliant. Red and green lie opposite each other on the color wheel and are therefore complements. Notice how green was used to shade the background flower. This green, complement of red, dulls the red and keeps this flower in the background.

Materials

Paints: (FA) = FolkArt Acrylics; (AP) = FolkArt Artists' Pigment Acrylics

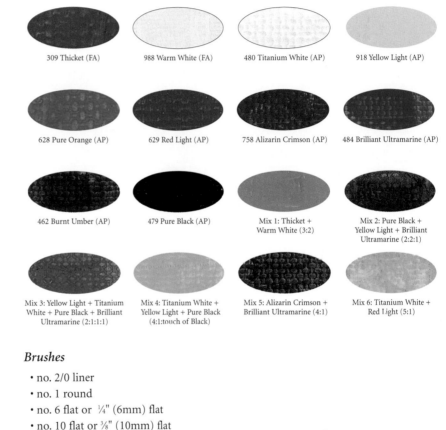

309 Thicket (FA)   988 Warm White (FA)   480 Titanium White (AP)   918 Yellow Light (AP)

628 Pure Orange (AP)   629 Red Light (AP)   758 Alizarin Crimson (AP)   484 Brilliant Ultramarine (AP)

462 Burnt Umber (AP)   479 Pure Black (AP)   Mix 1: Thicket + Warm White (3:2)   Mix 2: Pure Black + Yellow Light + Brilliant Ultramarine (2:2:1)

Mix 3: Yellow Light + Titanium White + Pure Black + Brilliant Ultramarine (2:1:1:1)   Mix 4: Titanium White + Yellow Light + Pure Black (4:1:touch of Black)   Mix 5: Alizarin Crimson + Brilliant Ultramarine (4:1)   Mix 6: Titanium White + Red Light (5:1)

Brushes

- no. 2/0 liner
- no. 1 round
- no. 6 flat or ¼" (6mm) flat
- no. 10 flat or ⅜" (10mm) flat
- 1" (25mm) flat wash
- ½" (12mm) mop
- 1" (25mm) foam

Additional Supplies

- 867 FolkArt Blending Gel Medium

Surface

- 11" x 14" (27.9cm x 35.6cm) book box from Viking Woodcrafts

This pattern may be hand-traced or photocopied for personal use only. Enlarge at 167 percent to bring up to full size.

Preparation

1   Remove the hinges from the box. Seal the entire box with wood sealer. When dry, sand the box with 400-grit medium sandpaper and remove sanding dust with a tack cloth. Paint the book box page edges with a thin wash of water, blending gel and Burnt Umber on the 1-inch (25mm) foam brush.

The addition of blending gel to the mix allows you to wipe off the stain to the desired shade (see photo on page 68). With the foam brush, basecoat the rest of the box with several coats of Thicket until well covered. Sand between coats.

Blended Background

2   To paint a lighter, blended background on the box lid, begin by spreading a very generous coat of blending gel and water on the lid using the 1-inch (25mm) wash brush.

3   Immediately paint a generous coat of blending gel and mix 1 thinned with water over the center area of the lid with the 1-inch (25mm) wash brush.

4   With Thicket on the brush, paint around the outside edge of the lid, then wipe the brush on a paper towel.

5   Blend the two colors where they meet by working the flat wash brush with a slip-slap brushstroke (as described on page 28) to begin. Then switch to straight horizontal and vertical strokes. Wipe the brush often as you blend the colors. Keep the center of the area lighter than the outside edges.

When the background is blended, soften the streaks of color with the dry mop brush using a light touch. The background will be somewhat splotchy. Let the surface dry thoroughly. A blow hair dryer will be an aid in speeding up the drying time.

Base Coat for Flowers

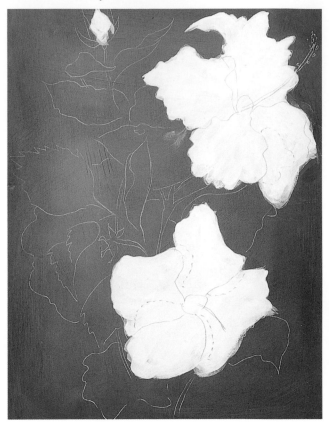

6 Transfer the pattern to the surface, using white or light gray transfer paper and a stylus. Basecoat the petals of the two main flowers and the bud with at least four coats of Titanium White. Do not basecoat the flower on the lower left of the pattern. Apply thin coats of paint to avoid leaving brush marks. When the basecoat is dry, transfer the flower details over the base coat with gray transfer paper or draw the lines with a pencil freehand.

7 Basecoat the flower on the left with three coats of Red Light on the no. 10 flat brush.

Left-hand Flower

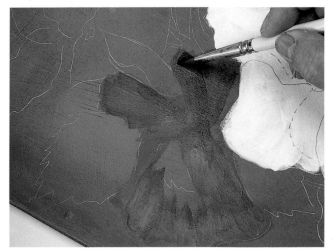

9 Continuing with the sweeping stroke, shade the petals with Alizarin Crimson. Then use Red Light on the no. 10 flat brush to form streaks of color on the petals. Lighten the flower with streaks of Pure Orange. Blend the colors very little as you paint.

8 Shade the petals with mix 2 on the no. 10 flat brush, using the sweeping stroke described on page 30. Work from the outer edge into the center of each petal.

Tip

The white base coat on the main flowers will show through the subsequent coats of red paint, giving these flowers a bright radiance.

Leaves

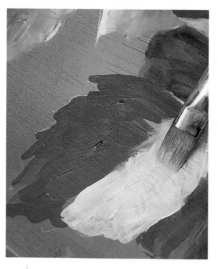

10 Retrace the pattern lines of the stems and leaves overlapping this flower with white transfer paper and a stylus. Or you may sketch in the lines with Titanium White on the no. 2/0 liner as I have done here.

11 With the no. 10 flat brush, paint the dark side of the large leaf on the left with mix 2. Pick up some mix 4 and paint the light side of the leaf.

12 Blend the two colors with the no. 10 flat brush using small slip-slap brushstrokes (see page 28). If the paint starts to dry, pick up more of either color needed. Blend until you achieve a smooth gradation of color.

13 Paint in a little Pure Black along the edge of the leaf with the no. 6 flat brush.

14 Blend the Pure Black with the other colors in the leaves. Paint the remainder of the leaves with mix 2 and mix 4, then blend as described in step 12. Add Pure Black to the darkest area of the leaves and blend. Use the image at left for placement of the light and dark values.

Leaves, continued

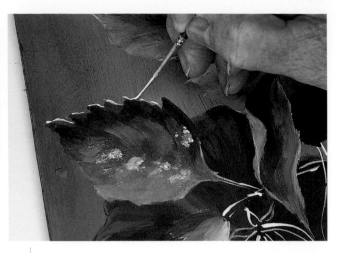

15 Highlight the large left-hand leaf by adding blending gel to the leaf first. Then brush streaks of mix 3 on the leaf, placing the light color between the spaces where the vein lines will be painted. Soften the streaks with the dry mop brush and let the leaf dry.

16 Paint the leaf with a small amount of blending gel, then dab on Titanium White reflections with the no. 6 flat brush. Soften only slightly. Continue to dab on Titanium White and soften until the center of the reflections are very bright white and the edges are soft and diffused. With the no. 2/0 liner, paint Titanium White on the edge of the leaf.

17 Highlight in between the veins of the other leaves with mix 3. Then add Titanium White reflected light to the leaves in the upper left. Paint the veins on all of the leaves with mix 4, using the no. 2/0 liner brush. Paint the green stems with mix 3. Darken areas of the stem with mix 4 and lighten the other areas with mix 2.

Branches

18 Paint the dark side of the branches with mix 5 on the no. 1 round brush. Paint the light side with Pure Orange. Highlight the branches with Titanium White.

Main Flowers and Bud

19 Basecoat the bright flowers and the bud with two coats of Red Light. Use the no. 10 flat and the sweeping stroke as described on page 30. Pull the strokes from the outer edge into the center of each petal.

20 Shade the petals with Alizarin Crimson, following the dotted lines on the pattern for placement. Use the sweeping stroke to pull the shading for each petal. Shade the bud as well.

21 Darken the shaded areas further with mix 5. Then paint some streaks in the darkest areas with the chisel edge of the no. 6 flat brush.

Main Flowers, continued

22 | With Red Light and the no. 6 flat, recoat the areas of the petals that were not shaded.

23 | Overstroke these highlight areas first with Pure Orange, then mix 6. Blend the colors slightly. With mix 6 on the no. 2/0 liner, outline the rippled edge of the top flower's petal.

Stamen

24 | Paint the stamens with Pure Orange on the no. 1 round brush, then highlight with Titanium White. Add dots of mix 5, Pure Orange, and Yellow Light on the end of the stamen.

For interest, add a hole in one of the leaves with Thicket.

Finishing

25 | Varnish the box with two coats of FolkArt Matte Finish Acrylic Sealer spray. Assemble the finished box with the hinges.

26 After varnishing, the reds and greens in this project are even more vibrant.

poinsettias

The technique for painting these poinsettias is much more involved than many of the other projects included in the book. This glazing technique takes several coats, a bit of time and some skill. However, since this book shows how to loosen up your painting style, it is not necessary to achieve perfection in your blending. If the shading and highlighting are a little splotchy, it will be well hidden when the veins are added.

You may use this tray merely for display, setting it in an arrangement or hanging it on a wall. Or you can use it as a serving tray for glasses that might be moist; if so, you will want to apply several good coats of polyurethane varnish to the finished project.

Materials

Paint: (FA) = FolkArt Acrylics; (AP) = FolkArt Artists' Pigment Acrylics

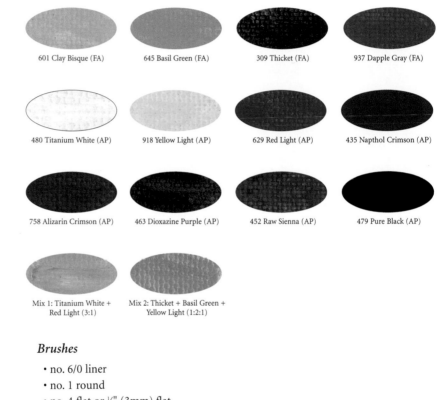

601 Clay Bisque (FA)

645 Basil Green (FA)

309 Thicket (FA)

937 Dapple Gray (FA)

480 Titanium White (AP)

918 Yellow Light (AP)

629 Red Light (AP)

435 Napthol Crimson (AP)

758 Alizarin Crimson (AP)

463 Dioxazine Purple (AP)

452 Raw Sienna (AP)

479 Pure Black (AP)

Mix 1: Titanium White + Red Light (3:1)

Mix 2: Thicket + Basil Green + Yellow Light (1:2:1)

Brushes
- no. 6/0 liner
- no. 1 round
- no. 4 flat or ⅛" (3mm) flat
- no. 6 flat or ¼" (6mm) flat
- no. 10 flat or ⅜" (10mm) flat
- 1" (25mm) foam

Additional Supplies
- 867 FolkArt Blending Gel Medium

Surface
- 14" x 21" (35.6cm x 53.3cm) wooden tray with wicker edging from Hofcraft

These patterns may be hand-traced or photocopied for personal use only. Enlarge the center design (at right) at 154 percent. The border pattern, below, appears here at full size. Repeat it as necessary around the tray.

Preparation

1. Seal the tray including the wicker edge with wood sealer. Sand the tray with 400-grit sandpaper, then clean off any sanding dust with a tack cloth. Paint the wicker edge with Raw Sienna thinned to a soupy consistency with water. Paint the floor of the tray with Dapple Gray on the 1-inch (25mm) foam brush until well covered, sanding between coats.

Tip

The red pigment in the acrylic paint is rather transparent. This makes it difficult to achieve a good solid coverage over the dark green. Painting the red areas with pink first will make it much easier to cover the area with the transparent red paint.

Border

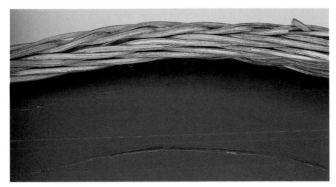
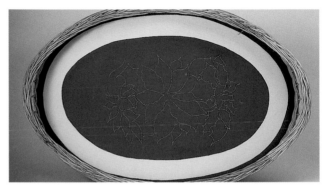

2. Measure ½ inch (1.3cm) from the edge of the tray and make a mark every 2 inches (5.1cm) around the circumference of the tray with a white chalk pencil. Connect the marks to make a continuous line for the border. Measure 1¼ inches (3.2cm) from the first line and make a mark every 2 inches (5.1cm) around the circumference. Connect these marks to make a line for the inside border.

3. Paint between the lines with Clay Bisque on the no. 6 flat brush until well covered. Use several thin coats and apply smoothly to avoid leaving visible brushstrokes. When dry, transfer the pattern of the poinsettia grouping to the center of the tray with white transfer paper and a stylus.

Base Coats

4. Basecoat the red leaves with at least three coats of mix 1 using the nos. 4 and 6 flat brushes. Keep the paint thin and the strokes smooth to avoid any visible brushstrokes.

5. Basecoat the green leaves with Thicket using the nos. 4 and 6 flat brushes.

6. With Red Light, basecoat the red leaves, again using the nos. 4 and 6 flats. Paint at least three coats for complete coverage.

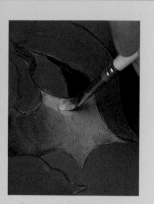

1 | When painting the pointed part of the leaves, start with the brush flat on the leaf.

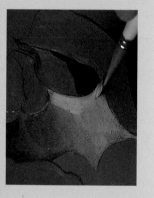

2 | As you pull the brush toward a point, lift the brush onto the chisel edge and fill in the point.

Green Leaves

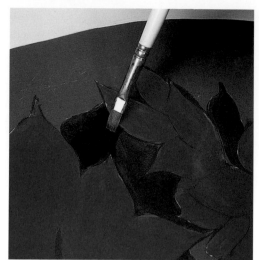

7 | Work on one leaf at a time in order to keep paint wet and allow blending time. Use the no. 6 flat or the no. 4 flat brush loaded with blending gel and Thicket (2:1) to coat the leaf. While the paint is wet, brush Pure Black onto the dark part of the leaf, generally the base or right side of the leaf. Blend this softly with the dry brush, using straight back-and-forth strokes, until smooth. Let the leaf dry.

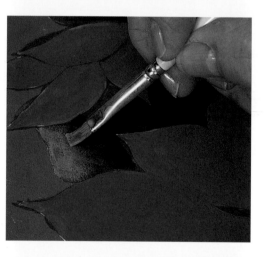

8 | Dampen the light part of the leaf with blending gel and Thicket (2:1) using the same brush. While the paint is still wet, brush mix 2 in the light area and blend softly in straight back-and-forth strokes to create a gradation from light to medium to dark values.

9 | After painting all the leaves with Pure Black and mix 2, apply a second coat of both colors to improve the coverage and allow a smoother blend. In this photo, the bottom right-hand leaves have been coated twice; the top center leaf has been coated only once.

Blended once

Blended twice

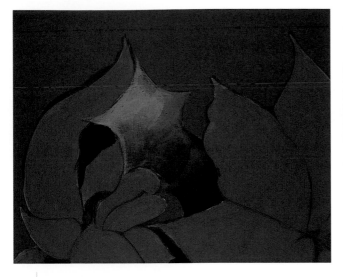

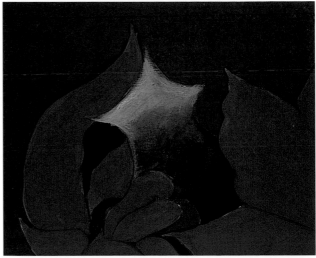

10 Recoat a few areas of the leaves with mix 2 and blending gel on the brush. While they are still wet, add tints of Red Light to the leaves.

11 Recoat the lightest part of some of the leaves with mix 2 and blending gel. Highlight these leaves with Titanium White. Let this dry, then repeat to make the gradation of color smoother.

Veins

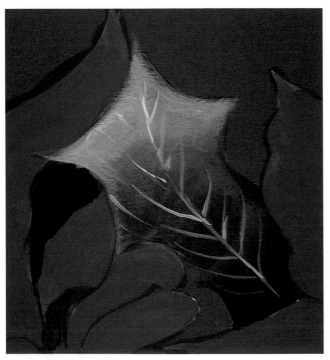

12 Paint the veins with the no. 6/0 liner brush and a mix of water and Basil Green. Work the paint well into all the bristles to allow paint to flow smoothly from the brush. (See the description of thin line brushstrokes on page 31.) Start the center vein at the base of the leaf and pull toward the point as you gradually lift the brush. Start the side veins at the center vein and pull toward the outside edge of the leaf, lifting the brush to a fine point. Highlight some of the veins with Titanium White.

Bracts

Shaded with Napthol Crimson

Shaded with Napthol Crimson and Alizarin Crimson

13 To shade the bracts (the red leaves on the poinsettia plant), recoat the parts of the petals that overlap other petals with Red Light and blending gel (refer to image in step 14 for shaded areas). Paint the shading of the cast shadow with two coats of Napthol Crimson, drying after each coat. Recoat the same area with Napthol Crimson and blending gel and blend in two coats of Alizarin Crimson, drying after each coat. In this photo the top petal has been painted with Napthol Crimson only. The bottom petal has been painted with Alizarin Crimson as well.

14 Shade all the bracts with Napthol Crimson and Alizarin Crimson as shown above.

15 The darkest shading will be a side load float of Dioxazine Purple. To side load the brush, dip one corner of the brush into the paint. Blend it out on the palette surface until there's a soft gradation of color that stretches halfway across the brush.

Shaded with Dioxazine Purple

16 With the no. 10 flat brush side loaded with Dioxazine Purple, shade the darkest areas. You will need two coats. Refer to the image in step 17 to see which areas have the darkest shading.

Dampen the highlight areas of the red leaves with Red Light and blending gel, using the no. 10 flat brush. Highlight the leaves with a thin coat of mix 1.

Veins

17 | Continue to add thin coats of mix 1 to build up the highlights. Dry thoroughly after each coat. Add more Titanium White to the mix for the final coat of highlights and place this lightest coat in an area smaller than the original highlights. The more coats you add, the smoother the highlights will be. The whitest area in the image was painted with five coats of Titanium White.

18 | Paint the veins with the no. 6/0 liner brush loaded with Alizarin Crimson thinned with water for the dark veins and Titanium White thinned with water for the light veins (see illustration above for placement). Follow the instructions in step 12 for painting the veins.

Flower Heads

19 | In the center of each poinsettia are tiny flower heads. Paint each flower head with Thicket on the no. 4 flat brush, then lighten with mix 2.

20 | Paint the top of each flower head with a mixture of Red Light + Yellow Light on the no. 1 round brush. Add a Yellow Light dot to each.

Side Groupings

21 | Complete the groupings of flowers on each end in the same manner as the center flower. However, notice that more of these leaves are shaded and the highlights are not as bright as on the center flower. The center flower is the center of interest and is therefore much lighter and brighter.

Border

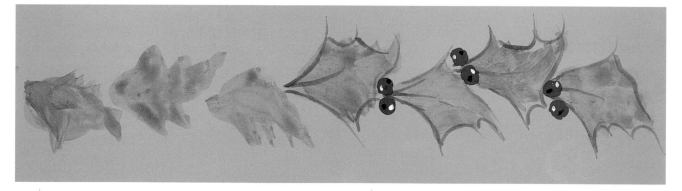

22 | It is best to paint the border freehand to keep the flow of the design. However, the pattern is given and you may transfer it on very lightly so you'll be able to cover your tracing with the thin paint. Paint the leaf shape with very thin Thicket on the no. 4 flat brush using the small leaf stroke described on page 31.

23 | Outline the leaves with slightly thinned Thicket on the no. 2/0 liner. Paint the berries with Red Light using the liner brush. Add a Pure Black dot on each berry, then add a Titanium White highlight dot.

24 Spray the tray with two coats of FolkArt Matte Finish Acrylic Sealer. This will be good protection for ordinary use, but it will not stand up to moisture from glasses. If you will use this as a serving tray, protect the painted surface with several coats of brush-on polyurethane varnish from a paint store.

sunflowers

*S*unflowers are the state flowers of Kansas, my home state. In the summer and fall they are everywhere—you can find them along the highways, in fields and wherever plants and flowers grow wild. There are several varieties and sizes. Most have the appearance of those in this project: unwieldy and untamed. They grow quite tall, reaching six feet or so, and most interesting are those with blossoms of a foot in diameter. They can be planted around the garden and look attractive hanging over a fence. It is this variety that is raised for the seeds.

The colors mixed for the flower petals are analogous, lying next to one another on the color wheel: yellow, yellow-orange, orange, red-orange and red. The blue-violet (in this case Brilliant Ultramarine paint) mixed with white makes a great complementary contrast with the yellow-oranges.

Materials

Paint: (FA) = FolkArt Acrylics; (AP) = FolkArt Artists' Pigment Acrylics

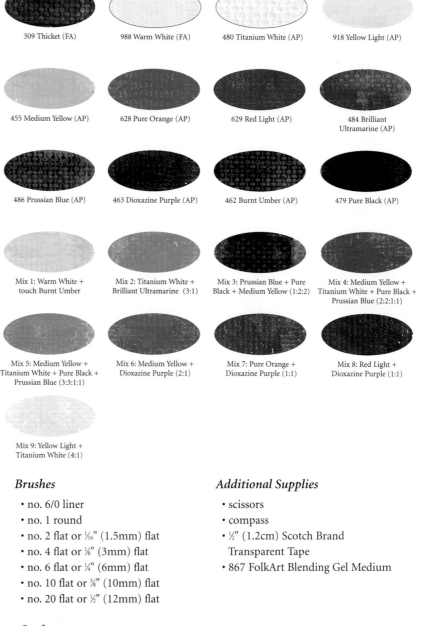

309 Thicket (FA)   988 Warm White (FA)   480 Titanium White (AP)   918 Yellow Light (AP)

455 Medium Yellow (AP)   628 Pure Orange (AP)   629 Red Light (AP)   484 Brilliant Ultramarine (AP)

486 Prussian Blue (AP)   463 Dioxazine Purple (AP)   462 Burnt Umber (AP)   479 Pure Black (AP)

Mix 1: Warm White + touch Burnt Umber   Mix 2: Titanium White + Brilliant Ultramarine (3:1)   Mix 3: Prussian Blue + Pure Black + Medium Yellow (1:2:2)   Mix 4: Medium Yellow + Titanium White + Pure Black + Prussian Blue (2:2:1:1)

Mix 5: Medium Yellow + Titanium White + Pure Black + Prussian Blue (3:3:1:1)   Mix 6: Medium Yellow + Dioxazine Purple (2:1)   Mix 7: Pure Orange + Dioxazine Purple (1:1)   Mix 8: Red Light + Dioxazine Purple (1:1)

Mix 9: Yellow Light + Titanium White (4:1)

Brushes
- no. 6/0 liner
- no. 1 round
- no. 2 flat or ¹⁄₁₆" (1.5mm) flat
- no. 4 flat or ⅛" (3mm) flat
- no. 6 flat or ¼" (6mm) flat
- no. 10 flat or ⅜" (10mm) flat
- no. 20 flat or ½" (12mm) flat

Surface
- 18" (45.7cm) diameter and 6½" (16.5cm) tall round wooden box with lid from Viking Woodcrafts

Additional Supplies
- scissors
- compass
- ½" (1.2cm) Scotch Brand Transparent Tape
- 867 FolkArt Blending Gel Medium

These patterns may be hand-traced or photocopied for personal use only. Enlarge the main design at top at 200 percent to bring up to full size. The border pattern below appears here at full size.

Preparation

1 Seal the entire box with wood sealer. When dry, sand the box with 400-grit sandpaper and clean off the dust with a tack cloth. Stain the inside and outside of the lid and the box with Burnt Umber mixed with a plentiful amount of water and blending gel so that it is as thin as ink. With the no. 20 flat brush, paint this mixture onto the box and lid, working one small space at a time, then wipe immediately with a soft rag to the desired shade.

2 To find the center of the lid, place a sheet of paper under the lid, then trace with a pencil around the lid's circumference onto the paper.

3 Cut out the circle with scissors. Fold the piece of paper in half, matching the edges of the circle. Fold the paper in half again. The resulting point will be the center of the circle.

4 Place the folded circle on the lid, matching the edge of the circle to the edge of the box. The point of the paper is the center of the lid, so mark this spot on the lid with pencil.

Border

5 | Place the tip of the compass on the center point and draw a circle with a 9-inch (22.9cm) diameter. Draw another circle ⅜ inch (1cm) wider than the first circle and just outside of the first circle. This slide shows the outer two border lines traced onto the lid, but the instructions to do so are in step 6.

6 | To form the outer borders, use the compass again. Hold the point of the compass just outside the outer edge of the lid and place the pencil lead ½-inch (1.2cm) from the outer edge. Pull the pencil around the circumference of the lid using the tip of the compass as a guide. Draw the next line 1⅛ inch (2.9cm) from the outer edge, and draw the inner line 1½ inch (3.8cm) from the outer edge.

Lid of Box

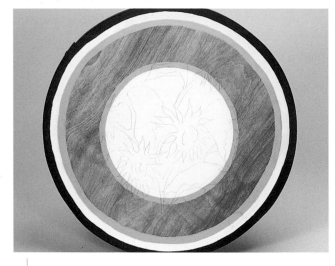

Leaves

7 | Basecoat the center circle with several thin coats of mix 1 using the no. 10 flat. Avoid leaving brush marks. Paint the next circular stripe with mix 2.

For the outer border stripes, work from the outside edge in to the center. Paint the outermost ½-inch (1.2cm) stripe with Thicket. Paint the next stripe with mix 1 and the next stripe with mix 2. Each stripe will take several thin coats of paint to cover.

Transfer the outline of the pattern onto the lid with gray transfer paper, matching the center X of the pattern to the lid center. You will be painting the leaves and stems first. You may obscure the flower pattern lines as you paint, so you may need to retrace these lines again before painting the flowers.

8 | Basecoat all the dark leaves with mix 3 until they are well covered. Use the no. 6 flat brush for the body of the leaves and the no. 1 round for the points of the leaves.

9 | With the no. 6 flat brush, pick up some blending gel with mix 3 and apply to some of the leaves again. While the paint is still wet, paint a lighter value green using mix 4 over the base coat. Pull the brush in the direction the veins grow in the leaves. Paint this lighter value on the large dark leaf in the upper left, a little on the leaf in the lower left, and on the right-hand leaf.

10 | Basecoat the lighter leaves with mix 4 using the no. 6 flat brush and the no. 1 round brush. Make sure not to paint over the pattern lines where a leaf folds or overlaps another. Basecoat the stems in the same manner as the leaves.

11 | Darken these lighter leaves with mix 3 mixed with blending gel. Use the no. 4 flat brush and pull the brushstrokes in the direction the veins grow in the leaf. Darken one side of each stem to give it round-ness. You will notice that the foreground leaves are lighter and the background leaves are darker. In places where a leaf folds, paint a cast shadow making the part behind darker.

12 | Using the no. 4 flat brush, pick up mix 5 and blending gel and highlight the leaves to show the overhead outdoor light hitting them.

Leaves, continued

13 To simulate reflections from the flowers, add mix 5 and mix 6—warm colors—to areas of the leaves that are below a flower. To simulate reflected light, pick up color mix 2—a cool blue—and paint parts of some leaves. Reflected light is usually placed opposite the highlight, but add some of the blue wherever you feel the leaves need enhancement, including on some of the stems.

14 With the no. 6/0 liner, paint the veins of the dark leaves with mix 4 thinned with water. Use mix 5 for veins on the lighter leaves. Loosely and lightly pull the center veins from the leaf base to the lower tip. Then add side veins that attach to the center. See page 31 for a description of thin line strokes.

Hole in Leaf

15 Outline a few leaves with mix 5, using loose, random lines just to give definition to some of the edges. Also with mix 5, highlight the stems on the left-most flowers.

16 Paint an insect hole in one leaf using the color that shows through from behind, in this case mix 3. Use the no. 1 round to paint an irregular shape for the hole.

Flower Petals

Tip

Painting the petals with the chisel edge of the flat brush will give a looser effect than painting with a round brush.

17 | Basecoat the petals of the pattern with one coat of Titanium White using the chisel edge of the no. 6 flat brush. Work from the inside center edge out to the tip of the petal, pressing the brush, then pulling and lifting as you make a stroke. Do this loosely so the outer tip of the petal will be ragged.

18 | In between the white petals, paint additional yellow petals with mix 6 on the chisel edge of the no. 6 flat brush. Pull the strokes from the center out to the petal edge. Begin adding strokes of mix 7 in between the white petals. Let some of these overlap the yellow petals.

19 | Continue to add strokes of mix 7, then paint some strokes with mix 8. Place these between the white petals and let the petals overlap.

20 | Basecoat the white petals again with one coat of Titanium White. Let these strokes overlap the yellow and orange petals some. Let dry.

Flower Petals, continued

21 | Paint over some of the white petals with a mix of Medium Yellow and blending gel. This is the medium value on the sunflowers. The center flower of the pattern is the lightest, so leave more of the white petals showing so the lightest value can be added later.

22 | Add a bit of Pure Orange to a few of the white petals.

23 | Now paint the remaining white petals with Yellow Light, the lightest value of petals.

24 | To soften the individual brushstrokes, mix a very thin wash of Pure Orange and water. Glaze over all the petals with the no. 6 flat. The effect is subtle, but it does soften the look of the sunflowers.

Flower Centers

25 | Fill in the flower centers with enough coats of Burnt Umber for complete coverage. Use the no. 6 flat brush, changing to the no. 1 round to paint around the base of the petals. As you do this, a scalloped shape is formed where the petals overlap the center.

26 | With the corner of the no. 6 flat, dab mix 6 on the centers to lighten them. Keep the very center of each flower dark. Load the no. 1 round with mix 6 and add a few dots around the center.

27 | Add more color to the flower centers with mix 7. Again use the no. 6 flat and no. 1 round, leaving the very center part open.

28 | Tap in just a few blue dots using mix 2 and the no. 1 round.

Final Petal Details

29 Lighten and clean up the base of the petals with more Titanium White and the no. 6 flat brush. Paint more white petals on the center flower because it is the center of interest. The light petals against the dark leaves will give the contrast necessary to draw your eye to this spot.

Leaflets

30 Paint the leaflet on the backside of the flower on the upper right with mix 4 on the no. 6 flat brush. Layer mix 3 on top.

Folded Leaf Details

31 Highlight this folded leaf with mix 5 using the no. 6 flat brush. Lighten further with Yellow Light and Titanium White. Reapply veins as needed with mix 5 on the no. 6/0 liner brush.

32 Loosely outline the inside edge of the leaf with mix 5 and the outside edge with mix 2. Use the no. 6/0 liner brush.

Side of Box

33 With a ruler, measure ¼ inch (0.6cm) from the bottom of the box and make a pencil mark at several places around the box. Draw a straight line to connect the pencil marks to create the first band around the box. Repeat at ⅜ inch (1cm) above the first mark, ¼ inch (0.6cm) above that mark, ¾ inch (1.9cm) above that mark, 1½ inches (3.8cm) above that mark and finally ⅜ inch (1cm) above the last mark. Working on one stripe at a time, mask off a stripe with tape along the pencil marks. Basecoat the stripes as follows, working from the bottom to the top: Leave the bottom stripe the original stain. Paint the next stripe Thicket. Leave the next stripe stain, then paint the next stripe Thicket. Paint the large stripe mix 1, then paint the top stripe with mix 2. For each stripe, apply several thin coats of paint to avoid leaving brush marks. Use the no. 4 flat for the narrow stripes and the no. 6 flat for the wider stripes.

Flower Border

34 Transfer the pattern for the flower head and leaf onto the side of the box. Repeat the pattern, spacing them 2¼ inches (5.7cm) apart. It is best to paint the stem without a pattern.

   Begin the flower with strokes of mix 7 using the chisel edge of the no. 2 flat. Pull the brushstrokes from the inside of the pattern circle to the outer edge. Overlap the brushstrokes. Basecoat the leaf with mix 4.

35 Add strokes of mix 8 to the flower. Darken the leaf with mix 3 thinned with water.

Flower Border, continued

36 Add strokes of Medium Yellow to the flower. Lighten the leaf with mix 5.

37 Add green strokes of mixes 4 and 5 to the flower. Paint most of these at the base of the flower head, but add a few around the head as well.

38 Highlight the flower with a few strokes of mix 9.

39 To some of the flowers, add strokes of Dioxazine Purple and mix 2 to the flower and the leaf.

40 Pull the stem of the flower using mix 4 thinned with water to an inklike consistency and the no. 6/0 liner brush. Then pull a short stem from the leaf to the main stem.

41 Repeat the flowers around the side of the box. Don't worry about making the flowers exactly the same—varying them will make them more interesting.

42 | Spray the box and lid with two coats of FolkArt Matte Finish Acrylic Sealer.

daisies

Materials

Paint: (FA) = FolkArt Acrylics; (AP) = FolkArt Artists' Pigment Acrylics

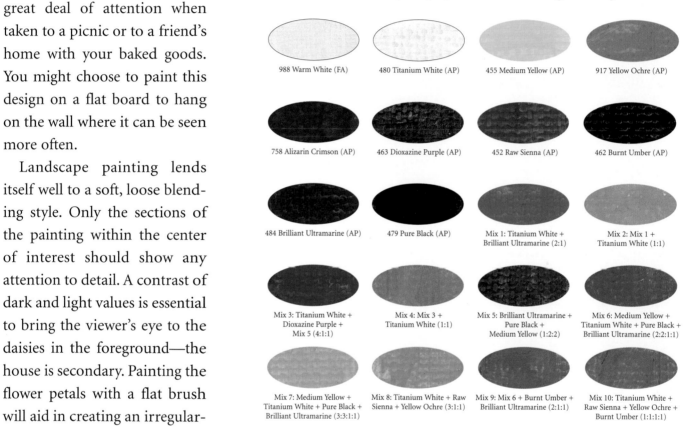

| 988 Warm White (FA) | 480 Titanium White (AP) | 455 Medium Yellow (AP) | 917 Yellow Ochre (AP) |

| 758 Alizarin Crimson (AP) | 463 Dioxazine Purple (AP) | 452 Raw Sienna (AP) | 462 Burnt Umber (AP) |

| 484 Brilliant Ultramarine (AP) | 479 Pure Black (AP) | Mix 1: Titanium White + Brilliant Ultramarine (2:1) | Mix 2: Mix 1 + Titanium White (1:1) |

| Mix 3: Titanium White + Dioxazine Purple + Mix 5 (4:1:1) | Mix 4: Mix 3 + Titanium White (1:1) | Mix 5: Brilliant Ultramarine + Pure Black + Medium Yellow (1:2:2) | Mix 6: Medium Yellow + Titanium White + Pure Black + Brilliant Ultramarine (2:2:1:1) |

| Mix 7: Medium Yellow + Titanium White + Pure Black + Brilliant Ultramarine (3:3:1:1) | Mix 8: Titanium White + Raw Sienna + Yellow Ochre (3:1:1) | Mix 9: Mix 6 + Burnt Umber + Brilliant Ultramarine (2:1:1) | Mix 10: Titanium White + Raw Sienna + Yellow Ochre + Burnt Umber (1:1:1:1) |

*T*his basket will attract a great deal of attention when taken to a picnic or to a friend's home with your baked goods. You might choose to paint this design on a flat board to hang on the wall where it can be seen more often.

Landscape painting lends itself well to a soft, loose blending style. Only the sections of the painting within the center of interest should show any attention to detail. A contrast of dark and light values is essential to bring the viewer's eye to the daisies in the foreground—the house is secondary. Painting the flower petals with a flat brush will aid in creating an irregular-shaped flower stroke.

Brushes

- no. 1 round
- no. 4 flat or ⅛" (3mm) flat
- no. 6 flat or ¼" (6mm) flat
- no. 10 flat or ⅜" (10mm) flat
- 1" (25mm) foam

Additional Supplies

- 867 FolkArt Blending Gel Medium

Surface

- 20½" x 14" x 9½" (52.1cm x 35.6cm x 24.1cm) wooden basket from Hofcraft

This pattern may
be hand-traced
or photocopied
for personal use
only. Enlarge at
169 percent to
bring up to
full size.

Preparation

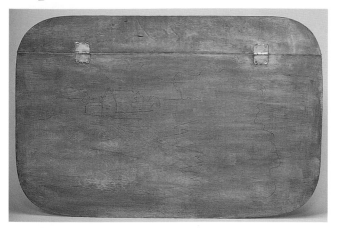

1 Remove the screws and remove basket lid. Seal the entire basket with wood sealer. Sand when dry and wipe with a tack cloth. Stain the basket and the lid with the 1-inch (25mm) foam brush and a very thin coat of mix 8 mixed with blending gel and water to a watery consistency. Stain the outer edges of the background on the basket lid with thinned Raw Sienna + Burnt Umber. Paint the top rim of the basket with Warm White. Trace the pattern onto the basket lid using gray transfer paper, leaving off the flowers and fence until the background has been painted.

Sky

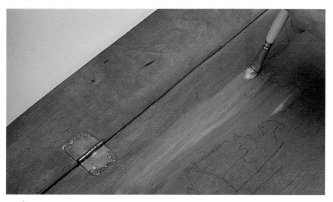

2 With mix 2 on the no. 10 flat brush, paint the sky with back-and-forth horizontal strokes. The thinned paint will create a streaked effect.

House

3 Paint the house with mix 4 on the no. 4 flat brush. Remember to use blending gel to keep the paint transparent.

Roof and Windows

4 Paint the roof and the windows with mix 3 on the no. 4 flat brush.

Note

Add blending gel to all the paint as you pick up each color. The paints will be transparent.

5 Outline the windows and trim with Titanium White using the round no. 1 brush.

Background Foliage

6 | Load the no. 4 flat brush with mix 5. Dab in the foliage around the house. Make some vertical up-and-down strokes at the sides of the house and some horizontal strokes on the horizon line.

Fence

7 | Paint in the tiny vertical lines of the fence along the horizon line using the no. 1 round brush and Titanium White.

Chimneys and Tree Trunks

8 | Load the no. 1 round brush with a brush mix of Burnt Umber and mix 1. Paint the two chimneys on the house and a few tree trunks in the foliage behind the house. These tree trunks are light to give a feeling that they are in the distance.

Grass

9 Begin painting the grass with mix 5 on the no. 6 flat. Paint horizontal strokes of grass in front of the house and along both sides of the road.

10 Overlap the dark value grass with the lighter value mix 6. Blend the two values together horizontally to give a smooth gradation of colors.

11 Paint and overlap the lightest value green with mix 7. Blend the colors again horizontally. Add more of this color to the left side of the road, and paint just a bit of it on the right side.

Road

12 Paint the road with mix 10 on the no. 6 flat brush. Lay the color on in horizontal strokes.

13 Add lighter strokes to the road with mix 8 on the no. 6 flat brush. For this color, add only a small amount of blending gel to the paint and leave the streaks unblended.

14 While mix 8 is still wet, paint in some horizontal strokes with thinned Titanium White, blending the two values. Since the light source in this design is coming from the left, keep this lightest value toward the right side of the road.

15 To further give the impression that the light is coming from the left, paint cast shadows to the right of where the tall grass will be on the left side of the road. Use mix 9 on the no. 6 flat brush to paint these shadows. Paint a shadowed effect across the lower part of the road as well so that the lower part of the entire painting is darker than the upper part.

Grass and Flowers on Left Side

16 | Use the chisel edge of the no. 4 flat brush to paint vertical streaks of grass with mix 5. Paint the strokes shorter in the background toward the house and increase in length as you move into the foreground.

17 | Load the no. 1 round brush with mix 5. Holding the back end of the handle of the brush, freely stroke in individual grasses, swinging the brush up, then down. These lines will be much finer than those made with the chisel edge of the flat brush. Load the brush with mix 6 and use the swinging technique to paint more blades of grass.

18 | Continue painting grass with mix 6. Layer these strokes, crossing some over others so the grasses look graceful and natural.

19 | Randomly paint tiny leaves in with the grasses using the no. 1 round brush and mix 5.

20 | Dab in tiny dot flowers of mix 2 with the corner of the no. 4 flat brush. While mix 2 is still wet, load the brush with Brilliant Ultramarine and dab in brighter flowers, occasionally working the two blues together. Dab in a few flowers with Alizarin Crimson. While the paint is still wet, dab in Titanium White flowers, working some into the red flowers for variety.

Foliage and Grass on Right Side

21   Dab in the foliage on the upper right side of the scene with mix 5 on the no. 4 flat brush. Cover the pattern line and go slightly beyond it with these strokes. Show more detail around the edges of this section with smaller and lighter strokes. In the center area lay on heavier strokes with more pressure on the brush. Dab some straight Pure Black into the center while mix 5 is still wet.

22   Fill in the remainder of the right side by scrubbing mix 5 onto the surface.

23   Using mix 6 on the no. 10 flat brush, make vertical brushstrokes with the flat of the brush. Lean the grasses to the right and some to the left. Keep the strokes loosely applied.

24   Make more defined grasses with mix 5 on the chisel edge of the no. 10 flat brush. Hold the brush near the end of the handle and swing up and down. Add more blades of grass with mixes 6 and 7.

Fill Flowers

25 Once the surface is dry, transfer the pattern of the flowers onto the surface with white transfer paper and a stylus.

26 Dab in the petals for the small blue flowers with mix 1 on the no. 6 flat brush. Follow the pattern lines for general placement, but then add a few additional petals to give the illusion of more flowers. Refer to page 31 for instructions on painting small petal strokes.

27 While mix 1 is wet, add Brilliant Ultramarine on some of the petals to brighten them. Add Titanium White to lighten a few petals. Paint a few strokes of mix 3 for some incomplete purple flowers.

28 Paint the centers of the three main blue flowers with Medium Yellow on the corner of the no. 6 flat brush. Dab in a few Titanium White fill-flowers with the corner of the same brush.

Tip

Painting the flower petals with a flat brush will ensure loose, natural-looking flowers instead of perfect, stiff-looking ones.

Daisies

29 Basecoat the daisy petals with mix 4 on the no. 6 flat brush. Pull the strokes from the edge of the petal toward the center.

30 Overstroke all the petals with one coat of Titanium White. Keep the strokes loose and the edges soft.

31 Overstroke the petals of the daisies in the foreground with another coat or two of Titanium White. Leave just one coat on the background daisies so that they are more muted.

32 Tap in the daisy centers with Yellow Ochre on the no. 6 flat brush. Highlight the centers with a few spots of a brush mix of Medium Yellow and Titanium White. Accent a few centers with Burnt Umber dots or a wash of Burnt Umber placed along the edge of the centers and around the base of the petals.

33 In areas with lighter-colored grass, paint the daisy stems and a few individual blades of grass with mix 5 on the no. 1 round brush. In areas with darker grass, use mix 7 to paint individual stems and grasses. Pull a few blades of grass across the road as well.

34 Spray the basket and lid with two coats of FolkArt Matte Finish Acrylic Sealer. Then reassemble the pieces of the basket.

wildflowers

One side benefit of painting is the information we gather and learn about the subjects we paint. The library book I used for these wildflowers gave me the names of the plants I was painting: The yellow flowers are black-eyed Susans, the white flowers are Queen Anne's lace and the purple berries are from pokeweed. I have seen all of these growing in wild conditions but I will now enjoy knowing the names.

The source of light is well established in this painting—it is coming from the upper left front. The flowers and leaves on the left are much lighter and brighter than those on the right. The highlight on the vase is left center and even the stems and berries have the highlights placed on the left side. The shadow of the vase is cast in the opposite direction from the light source.

Materials

Paint: (FA) = FolkArt Acrylics; (AP) = FolkArt Artists' Pigment Acrylics

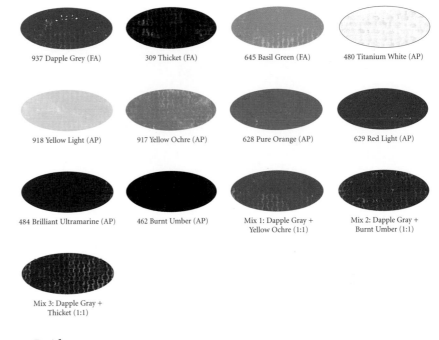

937 Dapple Grey (FA)

309 Thicket (FA)

645 Basil Green (FA)

480 Titanium White (AP)

918 Yellow Light (AP)

917 Yellow Ochre (AP)

628 Pure Orange (AP)

629 Red Light (AP)

484 Brilliant Ultramarine (AP)

462 Burnt Umber (AP)

Mix 1: Dapple Gray + Yellow Ochre (1:1)

Mix 2: Dapple Gray + Burnt Umber (1:1)

Mix 3: Dapple Gray + Thicket (1:1)

Brushes

- no. 2/0 liner
- no. 1 round
- no. 2 flat or ¹⁄₁₆" (1.5mm) flat
- no. 4 flat or ⅛" (3mm) flat
- no. 6 flat or ¼" (6mm) flat
- no. 20 flat or ½" (12mm) flat
- no. 6 bristle fan
- 1" (25mm) foam

Additional Supplies

- 867 FolkArt Blending Gel Medium
- T-square
- FolkArt Artists' Varnish satin finish

Surface

- 11" x 14" (27.9cm x 35.6cm) stretched canvas available from your local art or craft store

This pattern may be hand-traced or photocopied for personal use only. Enlarge at 125 percent to bring up to full size.

Background

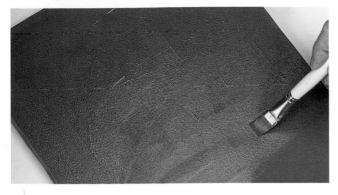

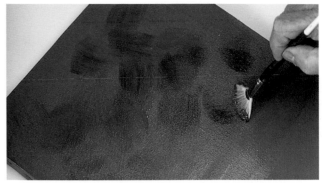

1 Paint the canvas with two coats of Dapple Gray using the 1-inch (25mm) foam brush. When dry, coat the top two-thirds of the canvas with a heavy coat of Dapple Gray and blending gel using the no. 20 flat brush.

2 While the paint is still wet, load the fan brush with mix 2. Make short sweeping slip-slap strokes, as directed on page 28, to apply the paint to the surface.

3 Soften the harsh brushstrokes with the no. 20 flat brush, but leave the background splotchy.

4 Paint the bottom one-third of the canvas with a heavy coat of Dapple Gray and blending gel using the no. 20 flat brush. Load the fan brush with mix 1 and apply the color with the sweeping slip-slap brushstroke.

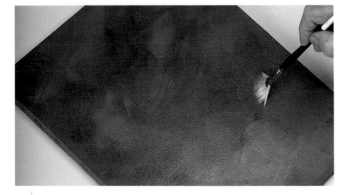

5 Blend this bottom third of the canvas with the top two-thirds, extending the bottom mix up and the top mix down. Dip the brush in a little water periodically to allow more open time for blending.

6 Add a few strokes of Titanium White to the bottom third to lighten this area further.

Background, continued

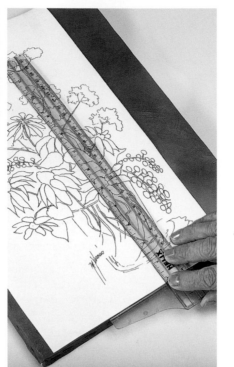

7 | Continue to blend until there's a smooth gradation of color, but keep the mottled effect. Dry completely.

8 | Place the pattern on the surface slightly right of center. To be certain the vase is straight, sketch a vertical line through the center of the vase. Then with a T-square, align the center of the vase perpendicular to the bottom edge of the canvas.

Vase

9 | Transfer the pattern with white transfer paper and a stylus. With the no. 1 round brush and mix 2, outline some of the vase, making the lowest edge of the curve in the center of the vase. With mix 2 on the no. 4 flat brush, paint the dark stems and reflections shown on the pattern and add more stems as well. Paint the cast shadow on the table with this same mix.

10 | Paint some of the stems inside the vase with thinned Thicket on the no. 1 round brush. Paint the rest of the stems with Yellow Ochre.

11 | Highlight the stems and the sides of the vase with Titanium White on the no. 1 round brush. Turn the surface so that you can pull the strokes toward yourself.

12 | Apply blending gel alone to the area where the main highlight is to be painted on the vase. Make one continuous stroke from the top down to the bottom of the vase using the no. 6 flat.

13 | With the same brush, dab some Titanium White to the top and bottom of the highlight.

14 | Then blend down and up between the highlights, pulling the color to form a transparent streak of light.

15 | Reinforce the white at the very top and bottom of the vase and blend slightly.

Tip

Painting on canvas has a way of softening the brushstrokes. The weave of the fabric does not allow for hard edges. Paint with rather transparent coats of paint because, while it takes more coats, it also results in uneven coverage and will loosen the effect. Remember you are looking for the finished overall effect and not zooming in on one leaf or petal— stand back to view the painting.

Flowers

16 *Queen Anne's Lace:* Lay in a base coat for the flower heads by painting the three white flowers on the left side with a small amount of thinned Basil Green on the corner of the no. 4 flat.

For the darker Queen Anne's lace on the right side, dab in the area of the blossoms with Thicket on the corner of the no. 4 flat brush.

Background: Fill in the dark area of the background around the three black-eyed Susans in the upper right with Thicket and the no. 6 flat brush. Add a few splashes of Yellow Ochre to break up the solid color.

Black-eyed Susans: The three flowers in the upper right are somewhat in the shadows and will be darker values than the black-eyed Susans in the foreground. Basecoat the petals of the background flowers with several coats of Yellow Ochre using the no. 6 flat brush.

17 *Queen Anne's Lace:* Paint in small splotches of very thin Titanium White on the corner of a no. 4 flat brush. Add a heavier coat of white to the flowers on the left side for more distinct blossoms. Add a few splotches of thinned Basil Green as well.

Black-eyed Susan: Add a thin glaze of Pure Orange to the petals with the no. 6 flat (see page 33 for instructions for glazing). Paint in the highlight with a brush mix of Yellow Light and a little Titanium White.

Tip

Paint the flower petals with a flat brush. This will avoid a stiff look to their shape.

112

18 *Stems:* Paint the stems with Basil Green on the no. 2/0 liner brush. Lighten the stems with Yellow Light. Paint the leaflets on the backward-facing black-eyed Susan first with mix 2 or mix 3, then with Basil Green using the no. 2 flat.

Black-eyed Susans: With the no. 6 flat, glaze over the yellow petals with very thin Dapple Gray to push these flowers into the background.

19 *Black-eyed Susans:* The four flowers nearest the vase are catching light from the light source and are, therefore, lighter and brighter than the upper flowers. Basecoat these four flowers with several coats of Yellow Light using the no. 6 flat brush.

Leaves and Background: With the same brush, paint the three small leaves above and to the right of the center black-eyed Susan with mix 2. Darken the center of each of these leaves with mix 3. Fill in the background around these flowers with Thicket as was done in step 16.

Flowers, continued

20 | ***Black-eyed Susans:*** Glaze the petals of these flowers with Pure Orange.

Pokeweed: Basecoat the pokeberries with Brilliant Ultramarine on the no. 2 flat and the stems of the pokeweed with Red Light on the no. 1 round.

Leaves: Lighten the outer edges of the three small center leaves with Basil Green on the no. 6 flat.

21 | ***Black-eyed Susans:*** With the no. 6 flat, glaze the underneath petals and the ends of some of the top petals with Dapple Gray. Lighten the top petals and the parts of the petals near the center with a brush mix of Yellow Light and a bit of Titanium White.

Pokeweed: Glaze the pokeberries with Burnt Umber on the no. 2 flat brush. Highlight part of the left side of the berries with thinned Titanium White using the same brush. Paint a more distinct highlight with thinned Titanium White on the no. 1 round. Highlight the stems of the pokeweed with Pure Orange.

Centers of the black-eyed Susans: Basecoat the centers with Burnt Umber on the no. 4 flat, then highlight the left side with thinned Yellow Ochre. Add spots to the centers with Red Light, Pure Orange and Yellow Light. The center on the far right is almost completely in shadow and therefore does not get any of the dots.

Leaves: Lighten the very outer edge of the three small leaves with Yellow Light.

Stems: Paint the stems for these flowers with Basil Green on the no. 1 round. Highlight the stems with Yellow Light.

22 | Coat the canvas with two coats of FolkArt
Artists' Varnish satin finish.

wild roses

$\mathcal{T}$he palette of mixed colors used in this project includes some good examples of adding a complementary color to dull a bright color. The pinks and greens in the project are mixed from red and green, which are complements on the color wheel. Mixes 3 and 4 are both made by adding green to red mixes, resulting in dull pinks.

The flowers and leaves are very loosely painted. The use of the no. 10 flat brush will not allow you to dabble in details. Paint only what is necessary and nothing more. Leave things somewhat undone and not blended smoothly. It is the overall effect at the end that is important.

Materials

Paint: (FA) = FolkArt Acrylics; (AP) = FolkArt Artists' Pigment Acrylics

309 Thicket (FA) 645 Basil Green (FA) 438 Ballet Pink (FA) 480 Titanium White (AP)

629 Red Light (AP) Mix 1: Basil Green + Thicket (1:1) Mix 2: Titanium White + Red Light (5:1) Mix 3: Titanium White + Red Light + Thicket (3:1:1)

Mix 4: Red Light + Thicket (1:1)

Brushes

- no. 6/0 liner
- no. 1 round
- no. 4 flat or ⅛" (3mm) flat
- no. 6 flat or ¼" (6mm) flat
- no. 10 flat or ⅜" (10mm) flat
- no. 20 flat or ¾" (19mm) flat
- ½" (12mm) mop
- 1" (25mm) foam

Additional Supplies

- 867 FolkArt Blending Gel Medium
- ½" (1.2cm) Scotch Brand Transparent Tape

Surface

- 9" x 9" x 3" (22.9cm x 22.9cm x 7.6cm) hexagon-shaped wooden box from Viking Woodcrafts

This pattern may be hand-traced or photocopied for personal use only. Enlarge at 118 percent to bring to full size.

Preparation

1. Coat the inside and outside of the box and lid with one coat of wood sealer. Sand when dry and wipe with a tack cloth. Paint the box and lid inside and out with Ballet Pink on the 1-inch (25mm) foam brush. When dry, use transparent tape to mask off the border space on the sides of the box. Paint the space between the tape with Basil Green. When dry, remove the tape.

Side of Box

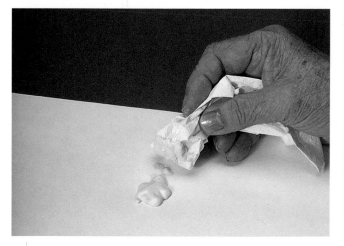

2. Wad up a paper towel and dip into the Ballet Pink.

3. Dab the paint onto the Basil Green band.

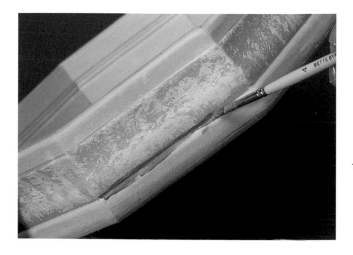

4. When dry, place transparent tape on the bottom edge of the border. Place another piece about ¹⁄₁₆ inch (0.2cm) below it. Paint between the pieces of tape with mix 1 on the no. 4 flat brush to form a green stripe. Remove the tape when dry.

Greenery and Leaves

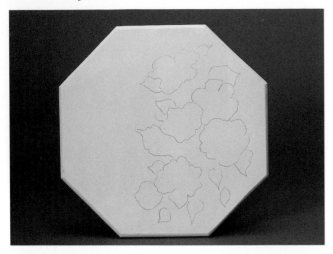

5 Transfer only the general shape of the blossoms and leaves to the lid with dark or light transfer paper. This will help with the placement of the background colors. If the pattern lines are heavy, wipe off some excess with a kneaded eraser. Spray over the pattern with spray sealer to retain the pattern while painting. While painting the background, the pattern will be obscured and you will need to trace it on a second time.

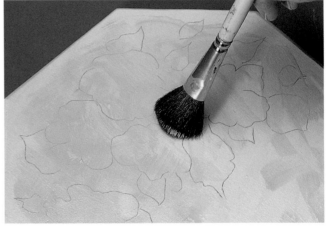

6 Heavily coat the lid with a brush mix of blending gel and water using the no. 20 flat brush. Load the brush with Basil Green and slip-slap the paint around the area in which the flowers will be painted. (See instructions for the slip-slap technique on page 28.)

7 Soften the brushstrokes with the dry mop brush. Wipe the brush often as you pick up paint.

8 Paint Thicket into the central part of the wet Basil Green area using the no. 20 flat brush. Again use the slip-slap technique to blend.

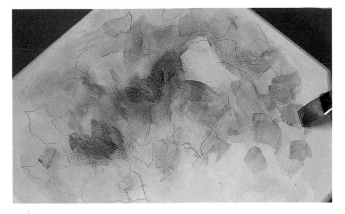

9 Soften the edges of the Thicket strokes with a mop brush. Thin mix 1 with water, and with the no. 20 flat brush, paint transparent shadowy leaves with indefinite edges along the outer edges of the background. Use the sweeping brushstroke, as described on page 30, for these leaves.

10 Paint smaller sweeping-stroke leaves with mix 1 on the no. 10 flat brush. Add a few gracefully trailing leaves at the ends of the design area.

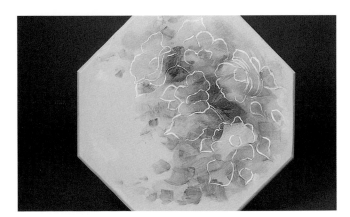

11 Let the background dry. Transfer the entire pattern except for details of the flower centers on to the surface with white transfer paper or sketch the pattern with Titanium White on the liner brush, as I did here.

12 Reinforce the Thicket shading with the no. 6 flat brush, dabbing the color to the left and below the cluster of three flowers. This very dark greenery will provide a strong contrast with the light pink flowers, creating a center of interest.

13 Paint some medium-value green leaves around the flowers at random with the no. 6 flat brush and mix 1. Fill in some of the pattern leaves with this mix as well. Use the smaller sweeping stroke as described on page 31. As you continue to fill in leaves in the background, be sure to paint out any transfer lines still showing. These cannot be removed after you have sprayed over the pattern.

Greenery and Leaves, *continued*

14 With Basil Green, the lightest green value, add more leaves and fill in some of the pattern leaves.

15 Shade a few leaves with mix 3, a dusty pink color, thinned with blending gel on the no. 10 flat brush.

16 Load the no. 6/0 liner with mix 1 and paint stems over the light areas of the greenery. Hold the brush straight up and down. Then flip the brush just a little as you move to paint the stem. This stroke gives the stems an irregular angular shape. Load the brush with Basil Green and paint the stems in the darker areas of the greenery.

17 Outline some leaves with the same mixtures and brushstroke. Purposely do not outline the exact edge of the leaf. A shadowy smudge can become a leaf and a few lines placed loosely around the "leaf" can form a leaflet.

18 To soften the greenery, glaze over the entire surface of the lid with a very thin wash of Ballet Pink mixed with blending gel and water. See page 33 for a description of the glazing technique.

Flowers

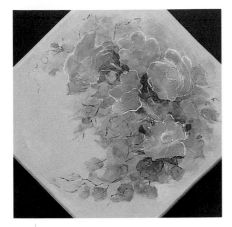

19 Basecoat all the petals with mix 3 on the no. 10 flat brush. Loosely follow the pattern for each petal as you basecoat.

20 Working on one flower at a time, paint the petals with mix 3 and blending gel. While the paint is wet, shade some of the petals with mix 1. Blend with mix 3 to soften the green.

21 With mix 4, paint a cast shadow wherever one petal overlaps another.

22 Highlight the light petals with mix 2 on the no. 4 flat, using the sweeping brushstroke as directed on page 30. Pull the stroke from the outer edge toward the center of the flower.

Tip

Use the glazing technique, described on page 33, for softening any part of any painting. Mix a small amount of paint with water or blending gel and glaze over the painting to blur the stiffness.

23 Paint the brightest highlight on some of the light petals with thinned Titanium White on the no. 4 flat brush. With paint that is less thin, paint Titanium White along the edge of some petals to give the illusion of a turned-up edge.

Flower Centers

24 | Reinforce some of the darkest patches of greenery with Thicket on the no. 1 round brush. Then paint dots of Thicket into the centers of the flowers with the same brush.

25 | Paint tiny stamens in the flower centers with Titanium White on the no. 6/0 liner brush.

26 | Paint tiny dots of Red Light on the flower centers with the liner brush.

Buds

27 | Paint the buds around the edges of the design with mix 3 on the no. 4 flat brush. Paint the calyxes with Thicket on the liner brush.

28 | Spray the box with two coats of FolkArt Matte Finish Acrylic Sealer.

Brushes

Bette Byrd Brushes
P.O. Box 2526
Duluth, GA 30136
(678) 513-6192

Paints and Mediums

Plaid Enterprises (FolkArt)
3225 Westech Dr.
Norcross, GA 30092-3500
(678) 291-8100
www.plaidonline.com

Surfaces

Hofcraft
P.O. Box 72
Grand Haven, MI 49417
(800) 828-0359
www.hofcraft.com

Viking Woodcrafts
1317 8th St. S.E.
Waseca, MN 56093
(800) 328-0116
www.vikingwoodcrafts.com

Walnut Hollow
1409 State Road 23
Dodgeville, WI 53533-2112
(800) 950-5101
www.walnuthollow.com

General Supplies

Designs From The Heart
for wood sealer
1218 Norman Dr.
Columbus, OH 43227
(614) 866-1521

Masterson Art Products, Inc.
for Sta-Wet Palettes
P.O. Box 10775
Glendale, AZ 85318
(800) 965-2675
www.mastersonart.com

Canadian Retailers

Crafts Canada
2745 29th St. N.E.
Calgary, AL, T1Y 7B5

Folk Art Enterprises
P.O. Box 1088
Ridgetown, ON, N0P 2C0
(888) 214-0062

MacPherson Craft Wholesale
83 Queen St. E.
P.O. Box 1870
St. Mary's, ON, N4X 1C2
(519) 284-1741

Maureen McNaughton Enterprises
RR #2
Bellwood, ON, N0B 1J0
(519) 843-5648

Mercury Art & Craft Supershop
332 Wellington St.
London, ON, N6C 4P7
(519) 434-1636

Town & Country Folk Art Supplies
93 Green Lane
Thornhill, ON, L3T 6K6
(905) 882-0199

U.K. Retailers

Art Express
Index House
70 Burley Road
Leeds LS3 1JX
0800 731 4185
www.artexpress.co.uk

Atlantis Art Materials
146 Brick Lane
London E1 6RU
020 7377 8855

Crafts World (head office)
No 8 North Street, Guildford
Surrey GU1 4AF
07000 757070

Green & Stone
259 King's Road
London SW3 5EL
020 7352 0837
greenandstone@enterprise.net

Hobby Crafts (head office)
River Court
Southern Sector
Bournemouth International Airport
Christchurch
Dorset BH23 6SE
0800 272387

Homecrafts Direct
PO Box 38
Leicester LE1 9BU
0116 251 3139

index

A
Acrylics. *See* Paints

B
Black-eyed Susans, 112-14
Blending gel, 12
Blending, 16, 28
Borders, 48, 78, 91-92
Bracts, poinsettia, 76-77
Brushes, 11
   care of, 16
   fan, 11
   flat, 11
   flat wash, 11
   foam, 11
   round, 11
   liner, 11
   mop, 11
Brushstrokes, 17
   Slip-slap for blending, 28
   Slip-slide for leaves, 29
   Sweeping for leaves and petals, 30, 32
   Sweeping for leaves and petals, small, 31
   Thin line for stems and veins, 31

C
Canvas, preparing, 14
Color
   complementary, 19, 21
   intensity, 21, 23
   intermediate, 20
   primary, 18
   secondary, 19
   value, 22-23
Complementary colors, 19, 21

D
Daisies, 94-105
Decorative painting society, 5
Drying, 16

F
Finishing, 16
Flowers, 101, 103
   daisies, 104-105
   hibiscus, 64-69
   pansies, 40-49
   poinsettias, 72-79
   poppies, 31-37
   roses, 55-59, 120-25
   sunflowers, 84-93
   wildflowers, 110-15

G
Glazing, 33, 123
Grass, 99, 101-102
Greenery, 41, 120-22
   See also Leaves

H
Hibiscus, 60-69

I
Impressionistic style painting, 9, 17
Intensity, color, 21, 23
Intermediate colors, 20

L
Leaves
   brushstrokes for, 29-33
   folded, 90
   holes in, 16
   pansy, 42-43
   rose, 57-58, 120-22
   hibiscus, 65-66
   poinsettia, 74-75
   sunflower, 84-86, 90
Loose-style painting, 9, 17

M
Materials, 10-13

P
Paints, 10
   mixing, 15-16
   white, 53
Palette, 12, 14-15
Pansies, 38-49
Patterns, transferring, 14
Petals, brushstrokes for, 29-32
   See also Flowers
Poinsettias, 70-79
Pokeweed, 114
Poppies, 31-37
Primary colors, 18
Queen Anne's lace, 112-13

R
Roses, 55-59, 120-25

S
Secondary colors, 19
Slip-slap brushstroke, 28
Slip-slide brushstroke, 29
Stems, 31, 35, 48
Sunflowers, 80-93
Supplies, 10-13
Surfaces, 13, 14
Sweeping brushstroke, 30

T
Tertiary colors, 20
Thin line brushstroke, 31

V
Value, color, 22-23
Vase, glass, 110-11
Veins, 31, 75, 77

W
Wild Roses, 116-125
Wildflowers, 106-115
White Poppies, 24-37
White Roses, 50-59
Wood, preparing, 14
Work area, preparing, 14

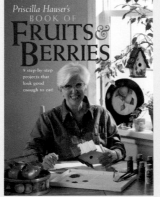
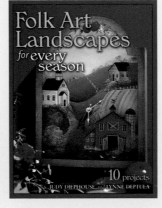

Phuong My Ly

CHIC KNITS
Stylish Designs from KNITPORT